# *Sartre and Psychology*

# STUDIES IN EXISTENTIAL PSYCHOLOGY AND PSYCHIATRY

SERIES EDITOR: KEITH HOELLER

**Published**

*Dream and Existence*

*Heidegger and Psychology*

*Merleau-Ponty and Psychology*

*Readings in Existential Psychology*

*Sartre and Psychology*

# Sartre
# and
# Psychology

Edited by

*Keith Hoeller*

Humanities Press
New Jersey

Originally published in 1980 as Volume XVII, no. 1 of
*Review of Existential Psychology & Psychiatry*

First published in this format 1993 by Humanities Press International, Inc.,
Atlantic Highlands, New Jersey 07716, and
3 Henrietta Street, Covent Garden, London WC2E 8LU

This edition © Humanities Press International, Inc., 1993

**Library of Congress Cataloging-in-Publication Data**
Sartre and psychology / edited by Keith Hoeller.
p.    cm. — (Studies in existential psychology and psychiatry)
"Originally published in 1980 as volume XVII, no. 1 of Review of
existential psychology & psychiatry."—T.p. verso.
Includes bibliographical references.
ISBN 0-391-03776-5 (pbk.)
1. Existential psychology.    2. Sartre, Jean Paul, 1905–
—Contributions in psychology.    3. Phenomenological psychology.
4. Psychoanalysis and philosophy.    I. Hoeller, Keith.    II. Series.
BF204.5S278    1993
150.19′2—dc20                    92-34508
                                 CIP

A catalog record for this book is available from the British Library

Humanities Press wishes to express its gratitude to the Minister of
Culture of the French government, who, with the help of the Office of
Cultural Services of the French Embassy, kindly provided a grant to
assist the publication of *Sartre and Psychology*.

Printed in the United States of America

# Contents

# Sartre &
# Psychology

# Introduction

KEITH HOELLER

> Man is nothing else but what he makes of himself. Such is the first princi-
> ple of existentialism. It is also what is called subjectivity, the name we are
> labeled with when charges are brought against us. But what do we mean
> by this, if not that man has a greater dignity than a stone or table? For we
> mean that man first exists, that is, that man first of all is the being who
> hurls himself toward a future and who is conscious of imagining himself
> as being in the future. Man is at the start a plan which is aware of
> itself.... But if existence really does precede essence, man is responsible
> for what he is. Thus, existentialism's first move is to make every man
> aware of what he is and to make the full responsibility of his existence
> rest on him. And when we say that a man is responsible for himself, we
> do not only mean that he is responsible for his own individuality, but that
> he is responsible for all men.... That is the idea I shall try to convey when
> I say that man is condemned to be free. Condemned, because he did not
> create himself, yet, in other respects is free; because, once thrown into
> the world, he is responsible for everything he does. The existentialist does
> not believe in the power of passion. He will never agree that a sweeping
> passion is a ravaging torrent which fatally leads a man to certain acts and
> is therefore an excuse. He thinks that man is responsible for his passion.[1]
>
> *Jean-Paul Sartre (1905-1980)*

The above citation is from Jean-Paul Sartre's "Existentialism is a
Humanism," a lecture given in October, 1945, and which marks, according to Sartre's bibliographers' Michel Contat and Michel Rybalka, "an
unforgettable day in the anecdotal history of existentialism."[2] The lecture
hall was so packed that people fainted and Sartre could barely be heard.
And although Sartre had never intended that the work be taken as a
fixed-in-stone introduction to his work, his publisher printed over
100,000 copies which were distributed worldwide.[3] Thus, through this
lecture (and numerous other works as well) Sartre became one of the
most widely read exponents of existentialism.

And yet, in popularized form, the sentences above do capsulize
many of Sartre's lifelong interests: in freedom, in the imagination, in
temporality, in responsibility both to oneself and to others, in choice and
action, and of course in human emotions and psychology.

Sartre's interest in psychology and psychiatry is present from the
very beginning of his studies. During the years 1924-29, while Sartre is
studying for the *agrégation* (French teaching certification exam) in
philosophy, he takes mainly philosophy and psychology courses.[4] His
first full thesis, written in 1926, is on the imagination, and it was published (in a different version, in 1936) as *Imagination: A Psychological Critique.*[5] This work, which serves as an Introduction to the later *Psychology
of Imagination*, critiques previous psychological theories of the imagination, and is indebted to Husserl's phenomenology (which Sartre had
studied in Berlin in 1933-34):[6]

---

> In any case, Husserl blazed the trail, and no study of images can afford to ignore the wealth of insights he provided. We know now that we must start afresh, setting aside all the prephenomenological literature, and attempting above all to attain an intuitive vision of the intentional structure of the image.... But eidetic description is the required starting point. The way is open for a phenomenological psychology.[7]

And relying on the principle of the intentionality of consciousness developed by Husserl, Sartre concludes that, "there are not, and never could be, images *in* consciousness. Rather, an image is *a certain type of consciousness.* An image is an act, not some thing. An image is a consciousness *of* some thing."[8]

But why should Sartre, the philosopher of radical freedom, have first written on the imagination? Sartre himself gives us the answer in a 1976 film, *Sartre by Himself*:

> *Contat:* What led you to write a graduate thesis on the subject of the imagination?
> *Sartre:* ...The idea that sensation was not identical to the image, that the image was not sensation renewed. That was something I felt in myself. It is bound up with the freedom of consciousness since, when the conscious mind imagines, it disengages itself from what is real in order to look for something that isn't there or that doesn't exist. And it was this passage into the imagination that helped me understand what freedom is.... Determinism cannot move to the plane of the imaginary.[9]

The imagination is a function of the freedom of consciousness and an indication of our ability to project ourselves into the future as well.

In 1928 Sartre collaborates on the French translation of Jasper's *General Psychopathology*.[10] And in 1934 he writes, while studying Husserl in Berlin, *The Transcendence of the Ego: Sketch of a Phenomenological Description*, which is published in 1937. In this crucial prelude to *Being and Nothingness*, Sartre critiques Husserl's notion of the "transcendental ego."[11]

During this time, Sartre is also writing and publishing psychological analyses embedded in his fiction, such as "The Childhood of a Leader" and *Nausea*.[12] And in 1939 he publishes *The Emotions: Outline of a Theory*, which is a part of a 400 page, still unpublished work entitled *The Psyche*.[13] This work analyzes classical and psychoanalytic ideas on the emotions, and offers Sartre's own phenomenological theory. For Sartre, the emotions represent a magical transformation of the world:

> We shall call emotion an abrupt drop of consciousness into the magical.... Therefore, it is not necessary to see emotion as a passive disorder of the organism and the mind which comes *from the outside* to

4

# INTRODUCTION

disturb the psychic life. On the contrary, it is the return of consciousness to the magical attitude, one of the great attitudes which are essential to it, with appearance of the correlative world, the magical world. Emotion is not an accident. It is a mode of existence of consciousness, one of the ways in which it *understands* (in the Heideggerian sense of "Verstehen") its "being-in-the-world".... It has a meaning; it *signifies something for my psychic life.*[14]

But this emotional level is not the same as a reflective consciousness, which can indeed be focused upon our emotions, though this is rarely done.[15]

Sartre's 1940 work, *The Psychology of the Imagination*, explores in greater detail the relation between consciousness and imagination, asking the question whether imagination is merely a characteristic of consciousness, perhaps one consciousness could do without, or whether perhaps wherever we posit a consciousness, we must also posit the imagination.[16] He concludes as we would expect:

There could be no developing consciousness without an imaginative consciousness, and vice versa. So imagination, far from appearing as an *actual* characteristic of consciousness turns out to be an essential and transcendental condition of consciousness. It is as absurd to conceive of a consciousness which would not imagine as it would be to conceive of a consciousness which could not realize the cogito.[17]

## EXISTENTIAL PSYCHOANALYSIS

It is this method which we call existential psychoanalysis. The *principle* of this psychoanalysis is that man is a totality and not a collection. Consequently he expresses himself as a whole in even his most insignificant and his most superficial behavior. In other words, there is not a taste, a mannerism, or an human act which is not *revealing*. The *goal* of psychoanalysis is to *decipher* the empirical behavior pattern of man; that is to bring out into the open the revelations which each one of them contains and to fix them conceptually. Its *point of departure* is *experience*; its pillar of support is the fundamental, pre-ontological comprehension which man has of the human person.... Existential psychoanalysis recognizes nothing *before* the original upsurge of human freedom.... Existential psychoanalysis rejects the hypothesis of the unconscious.[18]

Central to Sartre's *Being and Nothingness* is the idea of an existential psychoanalysis. But why? We have already seen how the imagination is bound up with consciousness and human freedom, and these concepts are no less important to Sartre's major work. For it is through our consciousness and imagination that we are able to make of ourselves what we are not; this is our human freedom, and it is a choice. "Freedom is precisely the being which makes itself a lack of being."[19] This freedom however, takes place in the world as a being-in-the-world. The purpose

5

of an existential psychoanalysis is therefore "...to determine the *original choice.*"[20]

> Since what the method seeks is a *choice of being* at the same time as a *being*, it must reduce particular behavior patterns to fundamental relations—not of sexuality or of the will to power, but of *being*—which are expressed in this behavior. It is then guided from the start toward a comprehension of being and must not assign itself any other goal than to discover being and the mode of being of the being confronting this being.[21]

The example he uses is the question of why Flaubert became a writer, and it is the study of Flaubert who will occupy his last decade of work. In studying Flaubert, he seeks to show how a choice was made, in spite of Flaubert's thrownness and so-called predisposition. Desires alone cannot explain anything; neither can an appeal to environment.

In order to understand human beings, it is not enough to philosophize about human being in the abstract. Sartre's psychological analyses follow directly from his existential approach, and his attempt to find an appropriate method for studying people. In the Preface to the first volume of his Flaubert book, Sartre tells us that *The Family Idiot* is a logical outgrowth of his *Search for a Method*:

> Its subject: what, at this point in time, can we know about a man? It seemed to me that this question could only be answered by studying a specific case.... For a man is never an individual; it would be more fitting to call him a *universal singular*. Summed up and for this reason universalized by his epoch, he in turn resumes it by reproducing himself in it as singularity. Universal by the singular universality of human history, singular by the universalizing singularity of his projects, he requires simultaneous examination from both ends. We must find an appropriate method.[22]

This method, which continues to focus on the concrete person as a being-in-the-world, offers a further contribution to a truly existential psychology. At the heart of such an enterprise there must always be a respect for the person one is studying, as Sartre says in the Foreword he contributed to R.D. Laing and David Cooper's study of his work, *Reason and Violence*:

> I also believe that one cannot study, let alone cure, a neurosis without a fundamental respect for the person of the patient, without a constant effort to grasp the basic situation and to relive it, without an attempt to rediscover the response of the person to that situation, and—like you—I regard mental illness as the "way out" that the free organism, in its total unity, invents in order to be able to live through an intolerable situation. For this reason, I place the highest value on your researches, in particular on the study you are making of the family as a group and as a series—and

6

# INTRODUCTION

I am convinced that your efforts will bring closer the day when
psychiatry will, at last, become a truly *human* psychiatry.[23]

## SARTRE AND PSYCHOLOGY

In this special issue on *Sartre and Psychology*, the Review is glad to
present several contributions in honor of Jean-Paul Sartre and his influence on existential and phenomenological psychology.[24] In "Music,
Meaning & Madness: A Conversation with Sartre," which appears here
in English for the first time in a translation by Debra Kelley, Sartre
reveals himself to Lucien Malson as a lifelong student of piano, and
discusses the nature of music and its relation to social class, and the relation of words to music. Sartre says "I believe that music in effect signifies
nothing, but that it has its meaning.... At bottom, it has no political
aspect.... It cannot be revolutionary in the true sense of the word."
Writing, on the other hand, is political, engaged, committed.

Sartre disagrees with Freud's idea that music is sexual sublimation.
He feels, too, that Freud's concepts of Eros and Thanatos are too
simplistic, saying point blank, "I am not completely convinced of the existence of Thanatos." Sartre further discusses the relation of music and
madness.

In "Sartre, Laing, & Freud," Max Charlesworth gives a fine outline of
existential psychiatry, including an interview with R. D. Laing discussing
his own relation to Sartre. He also sketches the relation between Sartre
and Freud, and reports Sartre's own comments on his relation to Laing.

In "Sartre's Concept of the Self," Hazel Barnes discovers four ideas
of the self in Sartre. Using Sartre's study of Flaubert as an example, she
goes through these various notions of the self, and concludes with an
original assessment.

Sander Lee's "Sartre's Theory of the Emotions" examines an apparent split in Sartre between the emotions and rationality. He shows
how the early theory on the emotions is consistent with the later work.
Lee objects to what he feels is Sartre's low opinion of the emotions in
comparison to reason, and argues for liberating the emotions from
Sartre's characterization of them.

Using Sartre's *Anti-Semite and Jew* as an example, Joseph Catalano
pinpoints the various senses of good and bad faith thereby clearing up
some of the usual misunderstandings with these words. In opposition to
Freud, Sartre says we choose our neurosis. Catalano argues that within a
Sartrean model, some choices are better than others, although there are
no absolutely right ones.

Linda Bell's "Boredom and the Yawn" offers an original
phenomenological contribution through a fascinating concrete study of

7

the meaning of boredom and the yawn. With Roquentin from Sartre's *Nausea* as a model, she analyzes the many possible meanings of boredom and the yawn.

NOTES

1 Jean-Paul Sartre, "Existentialism Is a Humanism," in *Essays in Existentialism*, trans. Bernard Frechtman (Secaucus, NJ: The Citadel Press, 1965), pp. 36-41.

2 Michel Contat and Michel Rybalka, *The Writings of Jean-Paul Sartre*, Volume 1: *A Bibliographical Life* (Evanston: Northwestern University Press, 1974), pp. 132-33. I have not hesitated to rely on this excellent work for detailed bibliographical information. For secondary source information *see* François and Claire Lapointe, *Jean-Paul Sartre and His Critics: An International Bibliography* (1938-1975) (Bowling Green, Ohio: The Philosophy Documentation Center, 1975). For Sartre in English *see*, "Selected Bibliography: The Philosophy of Sartre in English," in Hugh J. Silverman and Frederick A. Elliston (eds.), *Jean-Paul Sartre: Contemporary Approaches to His Philosophy* (Pittsburgh: Duquesne University Press, 1980), pp. 240-73. *See also* C. R. Bukala, "Jean-Paul Sartre: A Topical Bibliography," *Review of Existential Psychology & Psychiatry*, Vol. XIII, no. 1 (1974), pp. 106-24.

3 *Sartre by Himself*, trans. Richard Seaver (New York: Urizen Books, 1978), p. 74.

4 Contat and Rybalka, *The Writings of Sartre*, Vol. I, pp. 05-06.

5 Sartre, *Imagination: A Psychological Critique*, trans. Forrest Williams (Ann Arbor: The University of Michigan Press, 1962).

6 Sartre, *The Psychology of Imagination*, trans. Bernard Frechtman (New York: Washington Square Press, 1966); Contat and Rybalka, *The Writings of Sartre*.

7 *Ibid.*, p. 143.

8 *Ibid.*, p. 146.

9 *Sartre by Himself*, pp. 25-26.

10 Contat and Rybalka, *The Writings of Sartre*, p. 40.

11 Sartre, *The Transcendence of the Ego: An Existentialist Theory of Consciousness*, trans. Forrest Williams and Robert Kirkpatrick (New York: The Noonday Press, 1957).

12 Sartre, *The Wall and Other Stories*, trans. Lloyd Alexander (New York: New Directions, 1948); Sartre, *Nausea*, trans. Lloyd Alexander (New York: New Directions, 1949).

13 Sartre, *The Emotions: Outline of a Theory*, trans. Bernard Frechtman (New York: The Philosophical Library, 1948). For a detailed discussion of Sartre's theory of the emotions, *see* Joseph P. Fell, *Emotion in the Thought of Sartre* (New York: Columbian University Press, 1965).

14 Sartre, *The Emotions*, pp. 90-91.

15 *Ibid.*, p. 91.

16 Sartre, *The Psychology of Imagination*, pp. 133-34; For an Husserlian view of the imagination in psychology, *see* Jeffner Allen, "The Role of Imagination in Phenomenological Psychology," *Review of Existential Psychology & Psychiatry*, Vol. XV, no. 1 (1977), pp. 52-60.

17 *Ibid.*, pp. 245-46.

18 Sartre, *Being and Nothingness*, trans. Hazel E. Barnes (New York: The Philosophical Library, 1956), pp. 268-70. For further discussions of Sartre's "existential psychoanalysis," *see* Hazel E. Barnes, "Introduction," in Sartre, *Existential*

*Psychoanalysis*, trans. Hazel E. Barnes (New York: The Philosophical Library, 1953), pp. 01-37; *see also* Rollo May, "Introduction," in Sartre, *Existential Psychoanalysis*, trans. Hazel E. Barnes (Chicago: Henry Regnery Co., 1962), pp. 01-17; *see also* Hazel E. Barnes, "A Psychology of Freedom," in her book, *The Literature of Possibility: A Study in Humanistic Existentialism*. (Lincoln: University of Nebraska Press, 1959), pp. 273-362.

19 *Ibid.*, p. 567. For a further discussion of the relation of Sartre's earlier works to *Being and Nothingness*, *see* Hazel E. Barnes' "Translator's Introduction" to *Being and Nothingness*.

20 *Ibid.*, p. 570.

21 *Ibid.*, p. 274.

22 Jean-Paul Sartre, *The Family Idiot*, Volume I, trans. Carol Cosman (Chicago: University of Chicago Press, 1981), pp. ix-x. *See also* Hazel E. Barnes, *Sartre & Flaubert* (Chicago: University of Chicago Press, 1981), "Introduction: Approaching *The Family Idiot*," pp. 01-13.

23 R. D. Laing and David Cooper, *Reason and Violence: A Decade of Sartre's Philosophy 1950-1960* (New York: Random House, 1964), p. 6.

24 *See also Review of Existential Psychology and Psychiatry*, Vol. XIII, no. 1 (1974), another special issue on Sartre.

# Music, Meaning, and Madness:
# A Conversation with Jean-Paul Sartre*

AN INTERVIEW REPORTED BY LUCIEN MALSON

*Translated by Debra Kelley*

*Malson:* For the first time, in the interview with Michel Contat, "Self-Portrait at Seventy," you revealed a fact of which your readers were for the most part ignorant. Only members of your close entourage, those who knew you best, were aware of the part that music has played in your life.

*Sartre:* It has been considerable—which is of course the reason for my not speaking of this in my works, or speaking very little. It is an almost personal relation. I took piano lessons when I was a very young child. Later, I abandoned it, for it no longer interested me. During my twelfth year, I resumed practice alone, or with my mother. At this time, I re-called the "notes"—I could still read them, but I didn't know the fingerings. I tried to re-invent them, slowly, by playing easy pieces, then more difficult ones, until at about eighteen I was able to play certain works almost accurately. I was up to some works of Chopin and Schumann, of Bach, Mozart and Beethoven, and eventually some difficult works which I doubtless interpreted rather badly, but which I could sight-read fluently nevertheless. So, I have had a solitary rapport with music. It was better, I think, to avoid having others listen to me, and I exerted this restraint upon myself. I kept this prudence, maintained this protection for myself and others for sixty-five years. But I always played the piano for two to four hours a day. It was not in order to make progress, but to learn new pieces, new songs, to understand musicians.

I would acquire a piece, put the score on the music stand of the piano and decipher it. I would quite rapidly perceive the melody, have a very distinct vision of the harmony, and I would come to live in relation with the music in this way, daily, up until the moment when my sight began to fail. It was this which kept me from continuing. One day, the staves were blurred. I was no longer able to play.

*M:* You have never thought of improvising?

*S:* Yes, of course. And I also wrote a sonata in the process, which I have lost. I do not know if it had any value. Probably none at all.

*M:* You have frequented concerts. Simone de Beauvoir speaks of your visits with musicians in her *Memoirs.*

---

*This interview originally appeared under the title, "Entretiens avec Jean-Paul Sartre," in *Le Monde*, July 28, 1977, pp. 10-11. The *Review* is grateful to *Le Monde* for kindly granting permission to publish this translation.

*S:* Yes, I frequented them. I would go to hear anything at all, provided that I liked it. For example, as much Debussy as Beethoven or Schoenberg. I sometimes brought myself into the domain of music. I had much sympathy for Berg and Webern, and a little less for their followers.

*M:* You liked jazz. Your article on the "Milk's Bar" in the journal *America*, in 1946, expressed a very sober view of the manner in which one grows to understand — that is to say, without ceremony.

*S:* Absolutely.

*M:* You are said to have often been "partying" in Paris in the "jazz cellars" after the Liberation. One hears these stories often.

*S:* Ah! That's hardly true. I rarely went there.

*M:* That made up part of your legend.

*S:* Right. In reality, I was never at the places where I was said to have been.

*M:* Jean-Paul Sartre, the cliché of yellow journalism, was stereotypically associated with jazz and the café Saint-Germain-des-Près. In response, you would listen to jazz on record.

*S:* Yes, often. But I had little knowledge in the area. My friends the Vians had an acquaintance which was much greater than my own. I listened to records at their home frequently. I liked jazz. Yes, I was fond of it, and I still am.

*M:* What do you listen to today?

*S:* Today, I no longer have a phonograph. Actually, I do have one, at Simone de Beauvoir's apartment, but I go out now less frequently than I did, and less often to her home. On the other hand, I have a radio and simply listen to "France-Musique." It is a curious station, depending upon its program directors and administrators, and its quality varies over time. Sometimes it is good, sometimes bad.

*M:* How do you judge it to be at this time?

*S:* Very bad.

*M:* Why?

*S:* There is too much "pop." There is an enormous amount of jazz as well — in my opinion, an excess. Not that I find that it is without merit — it certainly is not lacking merit — but it is presented over long stretches, and overall, without much choice. I think, for example, of the late afternoon magazine: sometimes it is interesting, at times not at all…. I like to be well informed. However, I find that the radio does not fulfill its role, which would be to expose the best of musicians both in jazz and

12

in classical music. This it does not do. And this station, on the whole, does not succeed at all.

*M:* In your opinion it does not do this. The director would surely respond that the music which is incontestable, notably the classical music which you love, always occupies the greater part of the programs.

*S:* Yes, but I believe that "France-Musique" is not at all what it ought to be. And everyone tells me this. I do not pretend that, proportionally, the classical music which I appreciate does not have a larger place than other sorts of music. But its role is changed from the moment when, as soon as one turns the dial at random hours, one hears other things.

*M:* Jazz or "pop," eventually. As far as I am concerned, I would mark an overriding difference between the two.

*S:* I, too, would note the difference. The one which I admire is jazz. "Pop," for me, insofar as it is music, almost does not exist, with occasional exceptions.

*M:* Traditionally, extra-european music has been introduced into the program. Do you find this inclusion equally negative?

*S:* Their arrival is a good thing. I often wonder whether the confrontation between these arts and those of Europe would not produce some important novelties. The difficulty will be to find a common code. I am personally fascinated by Indian and Chinese music. As an anecdote: at a Parisian piano competition this year, of seven prizes awarded women, six were given to Japanese women. Musicians of the Far East are actually playing European music, without forgetting their own. One could easily conceive of the inverse situation. Will this, one day, give rise to a synthetic liaison between many forms of music? It is impossible to offer a verdict on this matter. One cannot know what will happen. Unfortunately, meanwhile, these extra-european arts lack an audience, and will not be encountered except by a very small number—those who listen to "France-Musique."

On the other hand, to return to this station's tiresomeness, apart from this positive contribution, it is this so-called "new music," with its pieces without unity, which allows the quality of the station to slide downhill. They play it constantly and propagate it, supposing that this bludgeoning of the senses amounts to something, whereas it is worthless. It is not sufficient to bombard the senses, it is necessary to know why and how. One must know this in order to develop understanding. This genre of music derails the listener, especially the young listener who would be willing and able to go a bit further. Thus he is rejected by the mechanisms of consumption, as well as by "France-Musique." Those responsible for the programming have lost the idea of true music, and have addressed themselves to an audience which asks for nothing more.

*M:* They have sought a new listener without necessarily wanting to break with the old.

*S:* Perhaps, but without defining him, and unfortunately without finding him.

*M:* Studies have shown that the audience has grown.

*S:* In the battle of surveys, this result does not impress me. There has been a slight inflation of its public, but coming from the channels of those who content themselves with listening to a flood of sound. It would be necessary for the next administrators—because there will be others, necessarily—to renounce all of this up to a point, beginning anew from what has been done in the past, to find better solutions. I do not wish to incite a musical "reaction." I want contemporary art to be propagated without limitations. But I object to its being supported and presented without discretion.

*M:* According to you, the derailed listener falls back into the same routine of musical consumption. All the same, the music of consumption is what one hears principally, and almost exclusively on the so-called "popular" stations, not on the so-called "cultural" stations.

*S:* Yes. All the people whom we see passing in the street are capable of reading interesting texts which concern them more deeply—or let us say 98% of them. But these same men and women, for the most part, listen to nothing except this dreadful music of consumption which is worthless, and they unfortunately admit that it bores them. They are vowed to ignorance because they have been deprived of culture and are without musical curiosity. At times, on Sunday, I listen to this kind of abomination. Notice that I consider the existence of lamentable music as normal; the enterprise of the destruction of music as normal. I don't envision an epoch where only true literature, true music will be read or played.

*M:* Valid music or refined music, true music or the music of consumption—who will judge? Plato said, in the *Laws*: "The mistake is to consider that the pleasure of the amateur decides the greatest justice." He adds: "Music must be judged on its ability to give pleasure, but not always on the pleasure of first hearing." Was Plato expressing an elitism, or on the contrary, is he aware that music must be learned and that it is necessary to have an institution because, as he said in this regard, "The most beautiful art has no charm until after sufficient training?"

*S:* I think that he could have had a music school, that he would have wanted one, and I also think that for certain music at least, the goal would have remained to reach the greatest number of listeners. And quality could have existed in very different forms.

14

*M:* A second, and also an old question, which is expressed in the *Republic,* concerning the relations between music and society: "One cannot change the modes of music without overthrowing the fundamental laws of the State." This was the problem of the Nazi Stege and the Stalinist Jdanov. Each protested a music removed (by bourgeois degeneration) from the values of the people and the historical heritage of the nation. Must one, in your opinion, speak of music of the people or of the bourgeoisie and play more of one than of the other?

*S:* A very important question. I do not think that there is one type of society where one must play bourgeois music and another type of society where one must play proletarian music, supposing that it would be heard on these terms. On the other hand, I know that in a single society there exists a difference of attention and taste among social groups. For example, the proletariat is certainly less sensitive, has less occasion to be moved by music in general than the bourgeois listeners. There are fewer proletarian musicians by vocation. That is not to say that the bourgeoisie are naturally more talented musicians than the proletariat, but simply that in a given period of history it is always the bourgeoisie that constitutes the musical public. Notice, after all, where music is played. It is always in the most central regions of a city or urban complex, and where one pays dearly for seats, which excludes the working class listener. Apart from a few, the workers don't attend. Jazz and "pop" arrived to slightly break down the social barriers of class, to vault the social walls and to address themselves to both factions, but only in rare cases. Actually, the proletarian and peasant public is not musically cultivated, at least not in bourgeois countries such as our own.

It is necessary to take a closer look at what happens in nations with people's democracies. In Moscow, for instance, I attended a concert where Stravinsky was re-introduced after 20 years. This concert was much applauded. But what does it mean to re-introduce Stravinsky to Moscow? Was this the re-introduction in the recreation halls which are always connected with factories, rooms where conferences are held, where exhibitions take place, where the workers will avail themselves of these concerts? Or was this an offering of Stravinsky to an intellectual elite by those who represent it? I believe it was the latter overall—Stravinsky was given back to an intellectual elite.

*M:* It is the problem of the networks, of the channels of distribution and audition. But the other problem remains more difficult, more thorny—the one of knowing what certain musics express. Is a music perhaps proletarian or bourgeois in its spirit, conveying this in itself? Do you accept the idea that art, therefore a music, is the "emanation" of a social class, of the conflicts of a social state; that it has the power to be an accomplice of injustice or favorable to political progress?

15

*S:*   In my opinion it never gives rise to a reflection. It is evident that there is a rapport between the social situation of a time and its music, but this rapport cannot be understood in terms of a reflection. Just so, because this situation cannot be understood through that which is truly wordless, without an ensemble of words and of phrases rendering different societal structures accessible. Now words are altogether outside of music. At bottom, it is not the rapport between society and music which it is valid to study; it is more the relation of words to music. I want to ask: what does a verbal description of a society give, and what does music render? Can one consider this similar to a verbal description — less clear, less fine on certain levels, more, on the contrary, on others? Can one, without the identification with speech, hold this as a sort of sensible résumé of the society of an era?

Let us reflect upon all of this. That which we have come to know from the 17th or 18th century, is the music which was played then, and which is played for us still, in concert today. This music possesses at one and the same time a direct aesthetic value, and a value of retrospective information. In this music, there are procedures, habits of creating successions of notes in a certain manner, of making temporal successions, of ordering the elements in a concerto or a sonata. Briefly, there is always an ensemble which is not properly rendered in language and which gives its sense to the music of the epoch. That is, that one may certainly grasp a manner of turning towards the aristocracy, and of refusing the people in the work of Bach, for example, which was, after all, addressed to the bourgeoisie on the whole. In the second half of his life, it was no longer the princes which, in effect, gave him his livelihood, but the church, and this church was administered by the bourgeoisie. Bach was always maintained by the society where he made his first acquaintance — that is to say, in a world where the aristocracy ruled and where music was destined for this aristocracy and remunerated by it.

*M:*   What you have come to say in a sense contradicts the formula of Stravinsky so often cited, and which I recall from memory: "I regard music, in its essence, as impotent to express anything whatsoever."

*S:*   I think that this is not true, and moreover, that Stravinsky expressed many things in his own music. He is the first to have contradicted his theory by his acts. I believe that music in effect signifies nothing, but that it has its meaning. The music of Bach does not pretend to draw an eighteenth century garden, or courtiers, or anything precise whatsoever, and as a consequence, does not depict the relations between things or persons either. It does not have signification at all, but it retains a meaning (*un sens*). A meaning is a very different matter. Music gives us a possibility of capturing the world as it was at each moment without object, without relation, but by a harmony which engenders it, and which offers it authenticity. The composer, having come to know the world by living in it, transports it, transposes it simultaneously into the work which he has created. What the ensemble of works of an era expresses is something which we all grasp without the power to define it well. This 'thing' is the meaning (*le sens*). Bach's music most certainly renders the meaning of the eighteenth century.

*M:* There is this meaning (*sens*) of an epoch for us who are elsewhere, and this is the formal beauty, the structural portent inscribed in the work. This is why one finds it difficult to understand the political ostracism in certain modern states with regard to certain musics of the past. I am thinking, in particular, of the recent tribulations of Beethoven in China: one moment forbidden, later rehabilitated. And who permits himself to decide in the name of the whole world, each time?

*S:* Those who permit themselves to decide are the people who come, who enter, and who leave. Beethoven was suppressed in China at one time, by virtue of an erroneous conception of music, in which Beethoven's work *uniquely* represents a kind of late 18th, early 19th century volatile magma such that, in the late twentieth century, there remains no alternative other than to suppress this phantom. It is an absurd thesis because Beethoven is obviously more than this. He surpassed the bonds of the 18th and 19th centuries. The quartets are not a reality which exhausts itself with the conflicts of the 18th and 19th centuries. Their reality still touches us, still concerns us. It surpasses the contradictions which it simultaneously manifests. The music of Beethoven is, in effect, the expression of the end of the 18th and the beginning of the 19th centuries, but it is at the same time something incomparably greater—a sort of view of this time which one may always have from the outside. A sonata of Beethoven composed in the 18th century expresses its time, and at the same time already is an almost exterior perception of that time. To recapitulate, we say that it is a vision of the 18th century from the inside, and a vision of the same from without. This is what a sonata of Beethoven is. And the last quartets are even more—a seizure of the music which will follow, of the sort which will develop later. It is a beginning; it is the history of a commencement.

*M:* It is an anticipation.

*S:* Yes. An anticipation.

*M:* You have written that there has been a "specificity of practice," notably musical practice, and an "irreducibility of spheres," whereby, according to you, there is an obligation not to reduce musical life to political life. You said this very precisely in the *Critique of Dialectical Reason.*

17

*S:*   Yes, certainly. One may admit that every form of activity, or that every man-made object is political in a certain sense. Music has also been political. Political in the sense that, for example, in the 18th and 19th centuries it was played either in the royal court, or before the general public. Naturally, it was not the same as a result. Music was accepted as it suited the place—that which was appropriate for the masses. Therefore, music was political, but not in an obvious way.

I will elaborate. A treatise is, in itself, political for all times. An essay by Mirabeau is political; it is such in the 18th century and in the 20th, even if, from the perspective of those reading with new tools, he says something different from his original intention. But this is not the case with music. It had the power to be political at the moment when the king took it to be suited for himself, or when the congregation believed that the music had been created for them. Music has the capacity to be political when it is played in the time in which it is composed. It is political in the sense that it accompanies, sustains, or reinforces discourse, or an action which unfolds itself at the same time as does the music, but it will lose this character twenty or thirty years later. Then, it is nothing more than music. This is important. It means that the political aspect of music is never more than *on loan* from the historical moment. At bottom, it has no political aspect.

*M:*   To return to the present, without offering the ensuing argument, it is sometimes said, as you know, that there is music which is politically "mobilizing," and that which is "immobilizing." In the past, you have asked: "How can you demand of a painter or a musician that he be 'engaged'?" As far as I can see, you have always thought this to be impossible.

*S:*   I do not think that this is possible. In any case, I don't believe it if one understands by "engagement," an engagement which is precise and concrete in a given society. I admit of an "engagement" in the sense that the great themes of a life, or of the lives of people lend themselves to being rendered by allusion, *by their sense (par le sens)*, in music. It is always possible to compose a symphony around the destiny of a person, or of Man, but not a symphony about the Fourth or Fifth Republic. No. There the "engagement" reaches its limit. Musical engagement is a very complicated issue. Can music say something, or not? That is the question of Stravinsky, to which we have not returned. But in the end, I believe it is necessary to pose another problem: I can see that music always expresses something, but at times it intends to signify, at other times it does not. There remain two possible attitudes for it. In any case, if Man is engaged by music, it is in the manner of revealing him to us in the midst of others and of nature; it is in its manner of dealing with death or with love. But music in itself cannot have a precise engagement in a given period. It cannot be revolutionary in the true sense of the term.

Realize, that when one reinterprets music without knowledge of the composer or without knowing what he wished to convey, when one hears a piece conceived 50 or 100 years previously, one always risks committing monumental errors. For instance, one may take a piece to be revolutionary when it was not, but was, on the contrary, a reactionary piece linked to a society in the process of degeneration. Again, music is not a tribunal discourse.

*M:* The great themes which music conveys in its sense are the relations with others, and above all, as you have put it, death or love. But if Freud is right, then this art would be, in the final analysis, nothing but a way of celebrating love by sublimation, or more precisely sexual love — "the prototype of our aspirations or well-being." Music, like all the arts, and by virtue of the themes which it conveys, plunges us into a "substitute satisfaction," a "consoling illusion," a "mild narcosis," and "alleviating tensions," gives us over to "play, without scruples or remorse, with our own fantasies."

*S:* It is certainly not in this way that we must define aesthetic satisfaction. It is necessary to define it properly, on its own terms, and not in relation to erotic satisfaction, even if it is said to be sublimated. For me, it arouses something completely different. I do not think of art, even music, in this way. This does not correspond to that which, in my experience, enables me to understand. There evidently are aesthetic sensations which have sexual impulses at their origins — this is indubitable. But the pleasure one receives in listening to the 9th Symphony of Beethoven is not sexual pleasure, not even sublimated sexual pleasure. So, what would this mean? If one held to the idea of an overcoming, it is an overcoming which is inherently musical which would figure into the pleasure.

Another point: there is, in Freud, not only Eros, but Thanatos, the death instinct. Eros, he says, is not only the sexual instinct, but the instinct of self-preservation as well, as in hunger. All of this seems too easy to me. At one extreme Eros, at the other extreme, Thanatos — and I am not completely convinced of the existence of Thanatos. Finally, as a slightly comforting, simplistic classification, Thanatos and Eros are all very well and good. But this does not truly illuminate artistic reality, musical reality.

*M:* All music does not equally manifest the sexual impulse which you observe in certain cases. There are those which do not seem to express this at all. There exists, on the other hand, music where the sensual element is vividly apparent. I am thinking of jazz, as you have guessed.

*S:*  I was going to say as much to you. Jazz is one musical form which has a very pronounced sensual, sexual aspect. This is true, but does not correspond at all with what Freud refers to, because one is given this aspect directly, not in a covert form or sublimated — one has it directly *as evidence.*

*M:*  In *The Idiot of the Family* you remark that European art was rational in the 18th century, and that in the 19th, or to date it more accurately, after 1850, art became neurotic. It became necessary to be neurotic, and sometimes even psychotic to succeed in art. And that continues. But you add: "It went from there to pathological writings, although the difficulties intrinsic to the use of linguistic signs rarely permitted them to be wholly beautiful." You are not speaking of music. It seems that it, too, would be jeopardized in madness, as with literature.

*S:*  It would be jeopardized, and the fact is that there is nothing in the experience of great composers, during the time when they were working, which produced signs of madness.

*M:*  All the same, Schumann, at the end of his life....

*S:*  Yes, Schumann, at the end of his life, but only at the end. And when one looks at the corpus of his work, at the renewed works, they are not truly psychotic at all. One tries to seize the psychotic moments, but that means very little.... Ravel, also, was insane at the end of his life, but he was, on the contrary, powerfully rational during the whole of his active and creative period. Music does not lend itself to being treated by madness. Obviously one could conceive a theme which would have "mad" implications, but if the music remains contemporary with the epoch in which it is played, there is a rationalism in the method, the musical function and the relation of notes; there is a rationalism which cannot be abandoned without bringing oneself to the point of cacophany. As a consequence, one can, indeed, have developments which are *a bit* "mad," but, if it is treated in a contemporary manner, it is not *truly* insane. It is a way of speaking of "madness" (*folie*), but not a manner of being insane. The same is true in literature, as well. In literature one speaks of "madness"; one is rarely insane.

*M:*  You listen to music "without notation." Do you think that it is going to replace scalar music?

*S:*  I don't know. I listen.

*M:*  What of computer music, that of Xenakis?

*S:*  Sometimes I like it, sometimes I don't.

*M:*  You listen to everything?

*S:* I don't like everything, but I listen to a little bit of everything. It would be desirable for the great majority of people to be able to play and listen to music. This would occupy very few leisure hours per day, spent in the practice of an instrument and in listening to "France-Musique" or to records.

*M:* Do you work while listening to records? Or while listening to the radio? Some people do this.

*S:* No. Either I listen to music, or I work. If one listens to music, one can hardly accord one's attention to doing something else. I do not think that one can be authentically in rapport with the music when one is seriously writing about difficult things where one's mind will wander and then one will resume. Music can only detract from the writing. Or vice versa. One cannot progress.

I just realized: we passed rather quickly just now over those musical forms which escape from the world of the note.

*M:* You like the world of the note.

*S:* Yes. When one speaks of musical materials, it is necessary to distinguish notes from groups of sounds. Between these two phenomena, naturally, there are many intermediaries. I want to say that of all musical forms, it is those dealing with notes that I prefer. There, I see the opportunity of grasping the tone as representative of all sounds, but placed on another plane. Pure tone is purified tone. It is the sounds of the world, purified. The point is not that I don't like "concrete" music, but it is difficult for me to assimilate, although I am successful in this. My problem is still to pass from the note to sound. What does this assume? That music is no longer a separate domain with a specialized material and removed from the world—it is the world itself. Ultimately, I am more attached to the airy, ideal realm of the note, than the pure materiality of sound. I don't know if I am right, but that is the way it is. This has come about, perhaps, by virtue of the fact that I studied music for sixty years in a period where these problems did not pose themselves. As a consequence, the note was, and remains, something privileged for me. At this time, where tone is divested of the note, sound has some tendency to ignite within me, but this does not quite come about. If, by chance, this were to happen, then the difference between sound, tone and note would disappear for my ear. But I am not to that point. Not yet.

21

# Sartre, Laing, and Freud*

MAX CHARLESWORTH

## I. EXISTENTIALISM AND PSYCHIATRY

Existentialism has had a profound influence upon psychiatry, mainly—to put it a little paradoxically—through the misleadingly called "anti-psychiatry" movement associated with the names of R. D. Laing and David Cooper in England, Maud Mannoni in France, Franco Basaglia in Italy, and Thomas Szasz and Rollo May in the U.S.A.

This "anti-psychiatry" movement (though in fact it is neither anti-psychiatry nor a coherent movement) took its origin in certain dissatisfactions with traditional institutional psychiatry. First, a dissatisfaction with its apparently materialistic and mechanistic view of the human psyche, man being seen as the product of blind instinctual forces and pressure operating within a given environment. Second, a dissatisfaction with the traditional definition of insanity or madness as a malfunctioning of the psychic mechanism, as though mental illness were analogous to physical illness. And third, a dissatisfaction with the way in which traditional psychiatry saw the relationship between the psychotherapist and the patient, the therapist adopting the role of the professional expert and viewing the patient as an inferior, someone to be cured by using a technique, rather than as someone to be confronted as an equal, person to person.

As against this traditional view of man, and of madness, and of the therapeutic relationship, the anti-psychiatrists have emphasized first that any psychic state, whether it be pathological or not, is symbolic—it signifies something beyond itself. Thus a neurotic is trying to tell us something by his apparently bizarre behaviour, and the psychiatrist's task is to try and decipher the *meaning* of that behaviour. In this sense, madness is not irrational behaviour for it is charged with meaning. Further, so-called mental illness is not to be seen as a malfunctioning of the psyche as physical illness is a malfunctioning of the body. Madness is rather a way of coping with an impossible situation or environment, a way of making an unlivable situation livable. And finally, the therapist and his so-called patient must have a person-to-person relationship. The therapist must give up his professional and expert role and must cease treating his patient as a kind of object-to-be-cured.

*This article is excerpted from Max Charlesworth's book, *The Existentialists and Jean-Paul Sartre* (New York: St. Martin's Press, 1976), pp. 42-55, 123-28. This book contains the text of two long programs, "The Existentialists" and "Jean-Paul Sartre," broadcast on the Australian Broadcasting Commission's Radio 2 early in 1975. The *Review* is grateful to St. Martin's Press for kindly granting permission for publication.

As Sartre has put it, "a 'patient's' cure has to begin with a face-to-face encounter and should subsequently develop into a joint undertaking in which each person takes his chances and assumes his responsibilities."[1] Any interpretation the therapist wishes to offer to the patient should be proposed "in the course of a long common adventure, in interiority, and not 'come' to him anonymously, like stone tablets." The psychiatrist, Sartre goes on, must seek "to establish a bond of reciprocity" between himself and the one he is caring for. Above all, he must respect in each patient his "mislaid freedom to act — as subject and as agent."[2] The American psychiatrist, Harry Stack Sullivan, expresses a similar view: "The therapist must become a participant observer, not a detached observer of the patient's life situation."

These ideas and attitudes, which are common to most of the anti-psychiatrists, have been formulated theoretically in rather different ways. Some, like Franco Basaglia, have drawn on Marxist categories, and an interesting group of Chinese psychiatrists in Shanghai have used Chairman Mao's dictum, "The leaders can turn for instruction only to those whom they lead," to argue that psychiatrists must learn from their patients. But many of the anti-psychiatrists have found the ideas of the Existentialists especially congenial, and they have turned to Sartre and Heidegger in particular and used their terms and categories to express what they want to say.

R. D. Laing and David Cooper in England, for example, have openly acknowledged the influence of Sartre's later philosophy upon their ideas. Laing's book on schizophrenia, *The Divided Self*, is full of Sartrean themes about the possibilities and limitations of our relations with what Sartre calls "the Other," and Rollo May and Daniel Yankelovich and others, such as the Swiss psychiatrists, Ludwig Binswanger and Medard Boss, have used the insights of Heidegger and his analysis of what he calls the "Dasein," the concrete human existent in the world.

The whole drift of Heidegger's philosophy is to try to overcome the separation of the self from the world, subject from object — the idea that we find expressed in its most dramatic form in Descartes' philosophy, namely, that I, this self, this conscious subject, exist in an inner private world, separately from, and over and against, the objective, outer, public world. Man exists, Heidegger says, as "a being-in-the-world," immersed, so to speak, in the world, and madness arises when this fundamental attitude of the "Dasein" is disrupted. Thus the American psychiatrist, Rollo May, says that "Existentialism is the endeavour to understand man by cutting below the cleavage between subject and object which has bedevilled Western thought since shortly after the Renaissance," and May's whole conception of existential psychoanalysis, as he calls it, is based upon this idea.

Our conscious life does not, as Descartes thought, constitute an inner, private realm of its own; rather, it is of its very nature directed outwards to the world. To think, for example, is not for some psychological process to take place within the privacy of my psyche; it is rather to be conscious *of* some object, and the same is true of all our conscious acts. They are object-directed, or "intentional"; they *ipso facto* involve us in the world outside ourselves. To be a conscious existent is to be open to the world, to be interested in the world, to be directed outwards to the world. And madness arises precisely when the human existent is no longer able to do this, no longer has an *interest* in doing this.

Descartes' view of the conscious subject, living in an inner, private realm of its own, is in fact, so Rollo May says, the very definition of madness. Much the same position is adopted by Medard Boss and the other practitioners of what they call "Daseinsanalysis."

In an interview with a Melbourne philosopher, Douglas Kirsner, and a psychiatrist, Dr. Murray McLachlan, I discussed the connections between Existentialism and psychiatry.

*Charlesworth:*  Douglas Kirsner, I know that you've made a special study of Existential psychiatry, and I wonder if you could give us some idea of the history and scope of the movement.

*Kirsner:*  The existential view of man really started with figures such as Kierkegaard and Nietzsche, who were against the prevailing nineteenth century century materialist and scientific view of man. The Existentialists have been very critical of Freud for his scientism, while also seeing that he had brought a good deal of insight about personality structure. I suppose you could say that the main criticisms of Freud by the Existentialists have been against his instinct theory and the other psychobiological explanations he gives for his psychoanalytical practice. The Existentialists are mainly concerned with unveiling the whole of the human existence rather than with being concerned with the disturbed functioning of a mechanism.

*C:*  So you see the development of Existential psychoanalysis as coming about by way of reaction against Freudian psychoanalysis.

*K:*  Yes, I do.

*C:*  Murray McLachlan, how do you see the relationship between Existential psychoanalysis and Freudian psychoanalysis? Is there all that much difference at the clinical level? What difference of approach would be involved, for example, if you were an Existential psychoanalyst as against being a Freudian psychoanalyst?

*McLachlan:*  I think the major difference is one of attitude towards the nature of the person we are concerned with. I see the Existentialist approach not as in any way incompatible with some of the traditional approaches, but addressing itself to another dimension of human experience. I see it in other ways as an expansion of our understanding of man and his existence, his experience, which deepens our comprehension of his state. It doesn't limit the understanding of man to abstract categories in the form of explanatory systems. It would, I think, suggest that these are only one way of comprehending the phenomena involved, perhaps a legitimate way to some degree, and on one level; but when we are attempting to understand the characteristic, the unique, aspects of human existence, we need to also incorporate this existential dimension to do justice to the fundamental aspects of human existence.

*C:* I suppose even to speak of Existential psychoanalysis is somewhat misleading, because it gives the impression that it is a coherent movement, whereas, I think you'd want to say, Douglas Kirsner, it's a very various and even diffuse kind of movement.

*K:* Yes, I would. Perhaps I could mention a few figures in the movement, and say something about their attitudes and influence. Karl Jaspers, for example, inaugurated an "understanding psychology" which emphasized the empathetic aspect, the idea of the intuitive grasp of another person's experience. According to Jaspers you can't really state objective laws about the relationship between two people, or about the sort of person somebody is, such as I think the Existentialists would probably say that Freud was doing.

*C:* And Jaspers has had some following, has he, in the field of psychiatry?

*K:* I think, interestingly, Jaspers has been very influential in the very traditional side of psychiatry; in fact, his general psychopathology is the standard framework for modern psychiatry.

*C:* Jaspers' compatriot, Martin Heidegger, has also had an enormous influence, through the so-called "Daseinsanalysis" movement.

*K:* Yes. Heideggerian "Daseinsanalysis" is the major existential, analytic movement in Europe, Ludwig Binswanger and Medard Boss, both Swiss analysts, being two of its most important exponents.

*C:* And then we would have to mention, I suppose, Jean-Paul Sartre, who derives from a rather different tradition, and has a rather different view on analysis.

*K:* Sartre's main contribution is different from Heidegger's. "Daseinsanalysis" was a movement based upon Heidegger's own thought, whereas what Sartre did in his early work was mainly to criticize Freud.

In his later work he has had a very large influence on the so-called "anti-psychiatrists" such as R. D. Laing and David Cooper and Aaron Esterson who have taken over his later categories about group interaction.

*C:* Murray McLachlan, Douglas Kirsner has been speaking about the influence of Heidegger, Jaspers and Sartre on Continental psychiatry. How about English psychiatry? Has there been any influence there?

*M:* Oh, certainly. Sartre's ideas particularly have been incorporated into the writings of Laing and Cooper, and recently Peter Lomas has been writing from a very original point of view, attempting to incorporate the insights of the European phenomenologists and Existentialists. In modifying many of the ideas of Sartre, Laing, for instance, has made certain assumptions, and made several statements or declarations, which in some way don't appear to do justice to Sartre's thinking. I think, for instance, that Laing takes up a position of privileged insight in regard to the nature of the society of which he would see consciousness being a reflection.

After my interview with Kirsner and McLachlan I was fortunate enough to be able to arrange an interview with R. D. Laing himself. Laing came to the B. B. C. studios in London straight from his clinic, and I was able to speak with him by radio-telephone.

*C:* Dr. Laing, your book *Reason and Violence*, written in 1964 in collaboration with David Cooper, was a kind of meditation on Sartre's two studies, *Saint Genet* and the *Critique of Dialectical Reason*, and you've said in your book, *Sanity, Madness and the Family*, that Sartre's ideas in those two works provided a theoretical background for your work on schizophrenic families. Now, I wonder if you could spell out in a little more detail exactly how you see the relationship between your own early work on schizophrenia and Sartre's Existentialist philosophy. Do you, for example, see a direct connection between the two, or did Sartre's philosophy simply provide you with a kind of arsenal of useful terms and categories?

*Laing:* Sartre's thinking, particularly in the *Critique of Dialectical Reason*, contained a number of theoretical terms which I found extremely useful in attempting to bring some theoretical order to the phenomena that I was studying in families. I don't think that what Sartre calls in that book his "totalization" contained especially new elements, but it was the comprehensiveness and coherence of this theory and the systematic working out of elements of it that I found so useful.

Anyone who is familiar with the literature of that time on the study of small groups from the inside would be aware that there was a great deal of looking around for models, a great deal of looking around for theoretical terms that would do justice to the phenomena that we were encountering. What I found lacking in the theories that were in the field, that were most relevant, was the element of what Sartre speaks of as the "dialectic," which I'm afraid I can't express in a few simple sentences because Sartre himself took the best part of half a million words to try and say what he in fact meant by that "dialectic." These theories used the model of a number of external objects in space, like billiard balls or the phenomena that are studied by physicists, to account for the interplay between the experience and the conduct of people when they are in something together.

Another aspect of Sartre's theory was that he made the point that it is not enough simply to think of the interaction between people in itself, but we have always to think of that interaction within the context of the social system in which one is embedded, and the embeddedness of that social system itself in other social systems, and the interpenetration of social systems within each other.

Another aspect of his thought which I found useful was the distinction he makes in his later writings between "process" and "praxis," between conceiving of events as simply happening without the mediation of any human agent, and as the result of human action. We may think of a human being after the model of a bio-computer and so on, but we can't really think of a computer as having the agency that a human being has. At that time, and even more so now, many people have been thinking that even the notion of human subjectivity and human agency is a sort of "anthropomorphizing," if you like, of man himself in a way which brings in a sort of ghostly residue of magical thinking into human affairs, the last remnant of the pathetic fallacy in thinking.

This view was expressed in the writings that were just beginning to appear at that time, in the fifties and in the later sixties, with the advent of different versions of French Structuralism, in the work of Michel Foucault and in the work of Lévi-Strauss and others. Sartre very much took objection to this work as obliterating "praxis" from the human scene. When Foucault in one of his books said that man as an historical subject is dead, this sentence reverberated around the European intellectual scene with something of the same resonance of Nietzsche's statement that God was dead.

At that time Sartre's work seemed to be a last — or if not a last, at any rate a very important — contemporary bastion for retaining a human theory of human beings.

I saw reflected in the psychiatric models, and brought to bear on extreme forms of human distress and suffering, an attempt to see what was going on entirely in terms of "process," confirming in a way the ordinary feeling that while people do act and initiate irreducibly from themselves a response to what comes their way, in certain extremities of human distress and suffering and breakdown the category of "praxis" no longer exists and has to be subsumed entirely within "process." It was, I saw therefore, an empirical illustration (I felt a very compelling one) of Sartre's general theory, that in order to avoid the pain and the conflict and the contradictions of the "dialectic," we attempt in our thinking and in our actions to pretend that there is, in fact, no interplay between agents interacting with each other, but only an interplay between some sorts of biomechanisms which possess no attribute of agency at all. Those at any rate were some of the foremost features of Sartre's thought that caught me at the time.

C: You don't see yourself then as a direct lineal descendant of Sartre; rather you've seen Sartre's work as a useful quarry for ideas and categories to interpret your own work.

L: Yes. In fact, Sartre was writing out of the same tradition that I'd been immersed in and swimming in for some while, and I felt that rather than being a lineal descendant, Sartre was a big vessel afloat in the same ocean that I was trying to keep afloat in myself. So I never regarded myself as deriving my position from Sartre. Again, by the time I came into contact with Sartre's later work, I was also rather older than I had been when I encountered his earlier work. His earlier work, particularly *Being and Nothingness*, had introduced me for the first time to Husserl. For instance, in the first chapters of *Being and Nothingness* he has considerations of the work of Hegel and Husserl, and I actually read *Being and Nothingness* before I'd read Hegel's *Phenomenology of Mind* and before I'd read Husserl. It was through Sartre then that I was impelled to get hold of Husserl and Hegel. Sartre's earlier work was newer to me and perhaps in a way more formative in the sense that it was a gate-opener to the tradition that Sartre espoused, Hegel, Husserl and Heidegger.

C: Despite the fact that you have drawn inspiration from Sartre's *Critique of Dialectical Reason* you don't appear to have been attracted by the version of Marxism that Sartre presents in that book.

L: I found Sartre's version of Marxism very useful in terms of his concept of "seriality" and also in terms of different forms or different stages of group formation. There is the non-organized group, which is what he calls the "pledged" group, and then the development of the organization, the structuring of the group, the development of permanent group-structures and the institutionalization of the group, and with that the inevitable component of structures that he calls "inertia."

I've never been attracted to Marxism in the narrow sense as much as I have been to the Marx who exists in that space whereby Lévi Strauss can say that no one nowadays — whether they're politically Left, Right or Centre, or in whatever brand of sociology and anthropology — can avoid in one sense being a "Marxist." But Marx's ideological position, and Marx's detailed economic analyses, and Marx's strategy for revolutionary action, belong to a different category, and none of these have I ever espoused in the same way that I've taken out of Marx and out of Sartre different aspects of thinking I've found useful to me.

Where I haven't been engaged in empirical research myself, I've never felt impelled to go too far in my own theorizing. I've never felt that it made any sense for me for instance to adopt, ideologically, a Marxist economic position, because I felt if I wanted to be an economist I would probably have to spend at least ten years in detailed factual study of the world's economy, and I would also nowadays probably have to be possessed of mathematical skills that I don't possess. So with respect to that side of Marxism, I've never been drawn to it, either in Sartre or in Marx.

*C:* I wonder if I could ask you a connected question. Let me cite to you a passage from a little book on your work and thought by Edgar Friedenberg. He says this: "His prophetic insights into the political character of first, mental illness, then of experience, have lead Ronald Laing to a position from which politics can only be seen as absurd." I don't know whether you agree with that or not, but the author seems to detect a sort of tendency in your thought to become progressively a-political. Sartre, on the other hand, has, of course, as we all know, become more and more politically committed.

*L:* I certainly take politics far too seriously to regard it as absurd, and I feel that politics, regarded as the ways in which our conduct and experience is subject to control by the group in which we belong, is not only a serious matter, but a necessary fact of living in any social system. I don't regard politics *per se* as a bad thing. I don't regard power *per se* as a bad thing. It would be as absurd to say power is a bad thing as to say that any other fact of our social life is a bad thing. It depends what the function of politics is.

There can obviously be vicious, brutal, barbaric and tyrannical and oppressive employments of power, and power can also be employed in ways that don't appear to be at all destructive but in fact the very opposite. I mean, you can talk about the "politics," say, of a symphony orchestra, which involves a common consent to take cues from the one leader, the conductor, whom we freely consent to follow only in so far as his leadership is in perfect time with the music that we're all playing and so enhances our common attempt to play it. In the post-revolutionary Bolshevist regime in Russia there were ideological objections, for in-

30

stance, to having conductors for symphony orchestras and there were attempts to play symphonies without a conductor which apparently didn't
succeed particularly well. It just depends how it's done and who's doing
it, and what are the economic and other self-interests being served and
who is exploiting whom.

But I don't think that it is necessary to suppose that in every social
system, the political component of it need be exploitative, and I believe
at any rate that in a Utopian sense it is possible to envisage a non-
exploitative politics.

I don't agree with Sartre that every intellectual should be actively
political in the immediate, and I doubt if he would mean that in fact.

*C:* Well, Sartre does suggest that an authentic psychotherapy is impossible in our present bourgeois capitalist society, since in the present
state of society, the relationships between the so-called therapist and the
so-called patient are inevitably falsified. I think Sartre would want to say
that we must have some kind of political revolution first of all, before
one can have an authentic psychotherapy, whereas I take it you wouldn't
agree with that.

*L:* Well, we can talk about an "authentic" or Utopian psychotherapy
that would exist in a Utopian world where no one was exploiting anyone,
although it would certainly be completely naive for any psychotherapist
to be practicing psychotherapy these days without an awareness of the
medical/political context in which psychotherapy is being conducted.

When I see people in psychotherapy, it is either clear before we start,
or I make it clear, that my understanding of my role as a psychotherapist
does not involve any political control, that is, should I say, any politics
applied to the patient outside of my room. In my room it's confined to
indicating that I don't want myself to be physically attacked, and I don't
want any of the elements of my room messed up, and at certain times of
the day, independent of where it is, I might indicate that it's not feasible
to carry on if the volume of voice is so loud as to disturb the neighbors or
other external, interested parties. But, apart from that, as far as I'm concerned, the other person in the transaction is a free man or woman,
although I am empowered by society to put people into hospitals whether
they like it or not. In fact, I've had some psychiatric colleagues who feel
that, when I see someone whom they would put into a hospital, I'm ab-
dicating my medical responsibilities to such a person by not putting him
into a hospital, whether he likes it or not. But I don't see that as authentic
psychotherapy, I mean that sort of coercive exercise of power over someone which he's not asking for; indeed, the very opposite.

So I am very acutely aware of the political environment, and also the
way in which that environment enters within the interstices of the

therapeutic relationship itself. But I don't feel that it is at all impossible to be a genuine person in this world with other people, even with all the things one can say against the social system. I believe that it is still possible to treat another person with respect, and to accord another person freedom, and to insist on being accorded respect and freedom on one's own part. I don't think that it is inevitable and necessary that we all transgress upon each other all the time because a lot of that is going on and a lot of that is in fact institutionalized within our society. I don't think that psychotherapy in our society is necessarily an exploitative activity, but I do feel that, in order for it not to be, the greatest of vigilance is required by both parties and that it is to a great extent an activity which swims against the tide. If both parties can do that swimming — and I think there are genuine psychotherapists — then it is possible.

I think psychotherapy is an activity that goes right back to the very roots of Western medicine, and it is in the fundamental tradition of Aesculapean medicine. It is a form of therapy and so is a human profession; it's one of the most profound professions there are. It's certainly as old as prostitution, and it's one that I think there's all the more need for, the more difficult the circumstances are. And it's all the more worthwhile in a social system that makes it all the more difficult.

*C:* I wonder if you've read Sartre's commentary on what he calls "the man with the tape recorder" in his book *Between Existentialism and Marxism*? Sartre draws a lesson from this curious incident that the Freudian conception of psychoanalysis leads the therapist to treat the so-called patient as an object to be observed and cured. Sartre therefore calls for new forms of psychotherapy in which, as he puts it, "there would be a bond of reciprocity between the therapist and the person he's treating."

*L:* I think that "bond of reciprocity" exists. There are therapists — whether they're Freudian or Jungians, or whether they call themselves one thing and another, or simply psychotherapists — who don't treat people as objects and as things, and who don't feel it is their job to impose their numbers and their scenarios and their values on the patient, but rather see therapy as a reciprocal undertaking and just don't have that impulse to depersonalize and reify the patient.

However, I think it is certainly true that psychoanalytic theory in some of its aspects is a depersonalizing and reifying theory. Freud is extraordinarily insensitive to this aspect of his metapsychology. From his own letters and his case histories and so on, he seems to have had a very human relationship with his patients. But when he came to *think* about it, he definitely seemed to feel that it was his scientific obligation to translate all that happened in human terms into terms of things. Thus when he takes the metapsychological theory of the mind and says, "Well, let's think of the psyche," (that's us as we feel, in experiencing, image, and dream and so forth) he considers the psyche as having parts so that we can think of one part, an "ego," and another part, a "superego." Actually, in German the terms that Freud uses as technical terms are ordinary colloquial German words which are very often stilted in their translation into foreign languages. For instance, a term like "cathexis": God knows what "cathexis" is, but in German it's the same word for sitting down in a chair, simply "besetzen." And when we're thinking in Freudian terms and translate as "ego," in German that's just "I." Again, when we talk about the "Id," again a Latin neologism, this is very different from Freud just talking about "it."

*C:* Dr. Laing, one last question. Apart from his influence on you, I think it's true to say that Sartre has never really caught on in England. Why do you think that is so?

*L:* Well, I wouldn't say he hasn't caught on. I would say "yes" and "no." He has had a very considerable influence on some aspects of English academia. But he has never caught on, say, in Philosophy Departments throughout the country. The philosophical élite in England, as we know, has always espoused, or has recently espoused more than anything, the tradition of Analytical Philosophy and Linguistic Analysis. Some of the most intelligent people in philosophy have had sufficient élan to keep that type of enquiry, which has very little time for Sartre, going as a live concern. And since, as I think always happens, the people who are the seniors have got the first chance of selecting out those of the juniors who don't agree with them, it's been kept a pretty well-closed shop.

However, there is in the British Isles a growing interest in phenomenology, the key-figures being Husserl and also Merleau-Ponty. And although Sartre perhaps isn't quite as central, he is being accorded increasing respect as a serious philosopher.

Another difficulty with Sartre is that the English academic tradition has never been politically "engagé" in the way that Sartre calls for very vociferously and I think a number of people are therefore put off by him. I think myself that this is due to the fact that maybe more than anything else, the United Kingdom has never been occupied in recent years. If British philosophers had had to live through a German occupation, if they'd had to take sides, if they'd had to go through all these agonizing choices and decisions and were really put in a position where they couldn't be neutral but had to be on one political side or another, then this would inevitably have affected their lives and hence their philosophy. I can't help feeling that there has been certain failure of sympathetic imagination in the past by the technical, professional British philosopher, so that even Bertrand Russell's political commitment was looked askance at. His political concern was regarded as a philosophical aberration.

## II. SARTRE AND FREUD

Sartre's long flirtation with Marx has been parallelled by his equally long love-hate affair with Freud. Sartre has explained how he was affronted at his first reading of Freud.

> I was incapable of understanding him because I was a Frenchman with a good Cartesian tradition behind me, imbued with a certain rationalism and I was therefore shocked by the idea of the unconscious. I must add that I remain shocked by what was inevitable in Freud—the biological and physiological language with which he underpinned his thoughts...[3]

Freud's basic idea that our actions are the product of dark irrational forces in the "unconscious," and that our real selves remain largely hidden from consciousness, goes completely counter to Sartre's view of man. It means that a large part of the human subject is seen, paradoxically, as a kind of "object" that can only be known from the outside, that is to say in the same way as we know other objects. For Freud, Sartre complains, I discover my real self very much as I discover objects in the world. Again, as with Marx, Sartre rejects Freud's scientific determinism and mechanism as being opposed to the human subject's essential freedom. If a man is not, as Marx pretended, the product of his history and the society of which he is part, neither is he the product of his biological and psychological antecedents, as Freud pretended.

At the same time, Sartre acknowledges the genius of Freud in bringing to light the essential purposiveness and symbolizing function of human consciousness. Even the most seemingly random acts have a purpose and meaning for Freud, and even the most trivial events of consciousness always symbolize deeper and more important realities. Seen from this point of view, Freud's theory of the psyche goes clean against any materialistic account which would see consciousness as a passive receptor of stimuli from outside. Unfortunately, Sartre complains, Freud formulated these insights in the deterministic and mechanistic language of nineteenth century science.

In *Being and Nothingness* Sartre's attitude to Freud is much more critical. Freud's theory of the unconscious is declared to be incoherent and Sartre shows that the "self-deception" which lies behind all personality disorders cannot be explained in terms of the Freudian mechanism of repression and the unconscious. Self-deception must in some queer sense be conscious and deliberate; we must know in some sense what we are hiding from ourselves.

> This is what has inspired a Viennese psychiatrist, Stekel, to depart from the psychoanalytical tradition and to write in *La Femme Frigide*: "Every time that I have been able to carry my investigations far enough, I have established that the crux of the psychosis was conscious." In addition the cases which he reports in his work bear witness to a pathological bad faith which the Freudian doctrine cannot account for. There is the question, for example, of women whom marital infidelity has made frigid; that is, they succeed in hiding from themselves not complexes deeply sunk in half physiological darkness, but acts of conduct which are objectively discoverable, which they cannot fail to record at the moment when they perform them. Frequently in fact the husband reveals to Stekel that his wife has given objective signs of pleasure, but the woman when questioned will fiercely deny them. Here we find a pattern of *distraction*. Admissions which Stekel was able to draw out inform us that these pathologically frigid women apply themselves to becoming distracted in advance from the pleasure which they dread; many for example at the time of the sexual act, turn their thoughts away toward their daily occupations, make up their household accounts. Will anyone speak of an unconscious here? Yet if the frigid woman thus distracts her consciousness from the pleasure which she experiences, it is by no means cynically and in full agreement with herself; *it is in order to prove to herself* that she is frigid.
>
> We have in fact to deal with a phenomenon of bad faith since the efforts taken in order not to be present to the experienced pleasure imply the recognition that the pleasure is experienced; they imply it in order to deny it. But we are no longer on the ground of psychoanalysis.[4]

In the latter part of *Being and Nothingness* Sartre proposes a new form of psychiatry based upon his analysis of "self-deception" and which does away with the Freudian notion of the unconscious. Sartre also claims that popularized forms of Freudianism have provided people with an excuse for "bad faith" or self-deception. After Freud, people excuse themselves for their failures by claiming that they are what they are because of their psychological antecedents: "Please do not hold me responsible for being frigid; I am what I am because of an unsatisfactory infantile attachment to my father," and so on.

Freud's form of psychoanalysis also, Sartre argued, put the therapist in a position of superiority *vis-à-vis* the patient, so that the so-called "patient" becomes an object to be observed and to be "cured." If the patient were suddenly to become a subject and demand to be treated as a subject, the whole Freudian technique of psychoanalysis would be disrupted. This is exactly what happened in a curious episode which was recorded and which Sartre subsequently published in *Les Temps Modernes* under the title of *The Man with a Tape-Recorder*. The report purports to be a real-life account of a session between a patient and his therapist. The patient suddenly produces a tape-recorder saying that he intends to record the session. At this the therapist, feeling his position of superiority threatened, reacts very violently, indeed quite irrationally. In fact, the more the confrontation proceeds, the more sane and rational the so-called "patient" appears, and the more irrational the therapist appears.

Sartre draws a number of lessons from the episode, the main one being that a psychiatric cure "has to begin with a face-to-face encounter and...subsequently develop into a joint undertaking in which each person takes his chances and assumes his responsibilities. He has been castrated? So be it. He certainly wants to be told this unpleasant fact, but by someone looking him in the face. The interpretation should be proposed to him in the course of a long common adventure, in *interiority*, and not 'come' to him anonymously, like stone tablets."[5]

*A:* Of course you have the right, and you're not backward in exercising it; many thanks.... You feel you're being accused; you're talking like an American who won't make a statement unless he has his lawyer with him.... Sit down!

*Dr. X:* I'm ready to talk to you and explain things to you.

*A:* Fine, let's carry on then!

*Dr. X:* But I'm not ready to talk in front of a tape-recorder.

*A:* But why were you just about to telephone?

*Dr. X:* Because I had told you that if you insisted on using a tape-recorder you had to get out.

*A:* But why? Why were you going to telephone?

*Dr. X:* Because I had told you that if you insisted on using a tape-recorder you would have to get out; I didn't want to have you put away, but....

*A:* But why did you.... You can't have me put away, you know! If anyone deserves to be put away, it's you—that's if we're trying to find out who's unbalanced.

*Dr. X:* I.... This really is....

*A:* Listen, I've got nothing against you. I don't want to harm you; on the contrary....

*Dr. X:* Right then, we're agreed. Turn off your tape-recorder.

*A:* This is fun, isn't it; except that I wish you'd stop being frightened....

*Dr. X:* I don't think it's fun.

*A:* But you're frightened. And your libido, what are you doing about that? Do you think I want to cut off your little willie? Of course I don't! I'm here to give you a real.... But it's fantastic! You've had this little occasion coming to you for a long time. Listen, admit that you're getting out of it very nicely. Doctor!!! Doctor, I've got nothing against you, but you obviously have...you've got something against yourself.

*Dr. X:* At this moment you're....

*A:* I've got nothing against you, but.... I feel you abuse your position. Yes, that's it. You have abused me. I would even go so far as to say that you've defrauded me, if we're going to use legal jargon: you haven't met your obligations. You don't know how to cure people — you only know how to make them worse. That's a fact — all we need do is ask your other patients, your "patients," or people you call your patients, people who come to you for help and get nothing, who get nothing but one long wait. Come on, sit down! Let's be reasonable. Let's be reasonable! There. Are you a man or a mouse? Are you a man?

*Dr. X:* For the last time, you've got a tape-recorder there and I won't put up with it.

*A:* I'm sorry. I have to repeat that I pulled this tape-recorder out — to use your words — because I didn't like the way you suddenly demanded that we drop the question of castration.

*Dr. X:* Well I'd certainly be willing to discuss the question of castration, if that is in fact your real problem, but I won't say anything in front of a tape-recorder.

*A:* Fine, well, we won't talk about it; we'll wait until you change your mind. You're trapped.

*Dr. X:* What do you hope to get out of trapping me?

*A:* I've got nothing to lose!

*Dr. X:* Maybe.

*A:* You're frightened! Come on now, Johnny. Buck up, eh? You don't want to?

*Dr. X:* You don't regard this as a serious situation.

*A:* It's terribly serious. That's why it would be much better if you'd put a different face on it than the one you are.... I'd have to have a nerve to let myself in for such a thing! Yet even so I need to be absolutely sure....

*Dr. X:* No, you don't have to be sure. If you were sure you wouldn't be acting like that! Now let me go; this is a highly dangerous situation.

*A:* Dangerous?

*Dr. X:* Yes, you're dangerous.

*A:* I'm not dangerous at all; you're only saying that. You never stop trying to make me believe I'm dangerous, but I'm not in the least bit dangerous.

*Dr. X:* You're dangerous because you don't have a grasp on reality.

*A:* That's not true.

*Dr. X:* You don't have a grasp on reality!

*A:* I'm a little lamb. I've always been as gentle as a lamb.

*Dr. X:* You don't have a grasp on reality![6]

Sartre ends his commentary on this confrontation, which he describes as a "tragedy of impossible reciprocity," by referring to a "new generation of psychiatrists (who) are seeking to establish a bond of reciprocity between themselves and those they are treating. Without abandoning anything of the immense gains of psychoanalytic knowledge, they respect above all, in each patient, their mislaid freedom to act as subjects and agents."[7]

The reference here to the "new generation of psychiatrists" is of course to those who, like R. D. Laing and David Cooper in England, have tried to put Sartre's ideas into clinical practice. In 1964, Laing and Cooper published a book called *Reason and Violence: A Decade of Sartre's Philosophy; 1950-60.*[8] This was a summary of and a commentary upon Sartre's work *Saint Genet* and the *Critique of Dialectical Reason.* Laing and Cooper's book hardly mentions psychiatry, but it is clear that they see in Sartre's analysis of society and social processes certain direct analogies with "schizophrenic families." Thus in his book *Sanity, Madness and the Family,*[9] R. D. Laing says that a good deal of the theoretical background to his study of eleven "schizophrenic families" comes from Sartre. Here, at all events, is Sartre himself on the relationship of his thought to that of Laing.

*Vicary:* Dr. R. D. Laing and his associates, and the whole of the anti-psychiatry school talk of the influence that you have had on their philosophy. What did you say that was relevant to the changes in psychiatry?

*Sartre:* I think that Professor Laing was looking for a theory which would put freedom first, so that mental illness, or what is known as mental illness, might appear as an aspect of freedom, and not as a disease resulting from a malfunctioning of the brain or from some physical complaint. I think what he meant is that within society, such as I conceived it, one could understand the nature of an aberrant but persistent attitude which at present is known as madness, an attitude that prevents a real contact with others and which is nevertheless a consequence of freedom. I think this is what Professor Laing is getting at. That's to say, a new conception of mental illness seen as a mode of life as valid as our own, but which, however, is likely to lead to total inertia, for instance, or to unbearable pain. He takes men as they are, not as mad men versus sane men, but as men; some reaching a certain stage of distress, others avoiding that stage. That is, I presume, what Laing seemed to want to take from my writings. As a matter of fact, I'm completely in favour of anti-psychiatry, such as it is practised by Laing and by others in Italy and France.

It is worthwhile mentioning in parenthesis that, despite his hostility to Freud, Sartre was for a time, in 1958-1959, engaged in a film on Freud directed by John Huston. Huston asked Sartre to write a script for the film and Sartre obliged with a vast work of some 800 pages. Huston and his aides cut and revised Sartre's script very drastically and Sartre then withdrew from the venture. "I broke with Huston," Sartre has said, "precisely because Huston did not understand what the unconscious was. That was the whole problem."[10] The film finally appeared in 1962 under the title, *Freud, The Secret Passion*, with Montgomery Clift in the part of Freud.

### NOTES

1 "The Man with the Tape Recorder," in *Between Existentialism and Marxism*, NLB, London, 1974, p. 201.

2 *Ibid.*, pp. 204-05.

3 "The Itinerary of a Thought," in *Between Existentialism and Marxism*, p. 37.

4 *Being and Nothingness*, pp. 95-6.

5 *Between Existentialism and Marxism*, p. 201.

6 *Ibid.*, pp. 204-05.

7 *Ibid.*

8 *Reason and Violence: A Decade of Sartre's Philosophy, 1950-60.* Tavistock, London, 1964.

9 R. D. Laing and A. Esterson, *Sanity, Madness and the Family*, Tavistock, London, 1964.

10 *Between Existentialism and Marxism*, p. 36.

# Sartre's Concept of the Self

HAZEL E. BARNES

The word "self" appears to mean all things to all people; it is often used in the vaguest possible way by psychotherapists who should know better. For some it is the hard kernel of unchangeability in a person, and for others it is an ideal to be realized. If Sartre's concept of the self has often been misunderstood, this is largely because he uses the same term to refer to different things in distinct contexts, which he himself keeps clear but his readers do not. Also, his emphasis on one rather than the other of these has changed as his interest and thought have developed. I should like here to do three things. First, I want to differentiate among various ideas of self as Sartre has defined them in his early theoretical work and to see how they stand in relation to his overall view of what the individual is. Second, I will consider what became of these theoretical formulations when Sartre, much later, set out to study the case of Flaubert. Third, by way of conclusion, I want to point up a paradox. At either end of Sartre's career readers have complained that somehow Sartre lost the living person. In *Being and Nothingness* (1943) the radically free and isolated individual seemed to be too little in touch with the everyday world to be real. All that remained was an abstract, impersonal consciousness. In *L'Idiot de la famille* (1971-72), by contrast, some readers were disturbed by Sartre's claim that every person is "a singular universal" (*un universel singulier*). Gustave Flaubert appeared to be only the *product* of his familial and societal conditioning. History demanded and in effect wrote the novels signed by his name. Suppose that we ask: Who *was* Flaubert? What would we mean if we were to answer, "He was himself"?

## I

There are three sharply defined usages of "self" by Sartre: first, the self of prereflective consciousness; second, the self as ego or as personality; third, the self as value. To these I am adding a fourth category of the self as embodied consciousness. Sartre himself is not inclined to use the word "self" to represent the total person as embodied consciousness, but clearly that is his goal when he wants to discover "what we can know of a man today...Flaubert, for example."[1] The "person" includes all of the first three notions of self, none of which can be wholly dissociated from the body. In *Being and Nothingness* he was concerned primarily with defining the ontological status of consciousness, ego, the body, their differentiation and their interdependency; the stress was always on consciousness. In *L'Idiot de la famille* ego and the body received far more attention.

41

## (a) The Self of Prereflective Consciousness

Every consciousness is a self-consciousness, Sartre declares, for consciousness is always aware of itself as consciousness. The self of prereflective consciousness derives from the fact that in being aware of an object, consciousness is aware of not being the object. To be conscious of a thing is to be aware that the awareness and the thing are not the same. For example, if there is suddenly a bright light, the immediate reaction is not that *I* am seeing a bright light; consciousness of the light implies that the light is somehow *there*, in front of consciousness, but not consciousness itself. I am referring, of course, to the famous "nihilation," of which Sartre makes so much. The human individual, whom he calls being-for-itself, is that part of being which effects a psychic withdrawal from the rest of being (being-in-itself). To nihilate is to be conscious *of* something as an object not identical with consciousness.

Thus there are two inextricable ingredients in any act of consciousness: consciousness *of* the object and a self-consciousness which Sartre indicates by putting the "of" in parentheses: *conscience (de) soi.* The latter is consciousness' awareness of itself as being aware. Sartre says that prereflective consciousness is personal in that there is a return to self, a slight displacement such as is indicated by some of the French reflexive verbs — for example, *il s'intéresse à...*(he interests himself in...).[2] The adjective "personal," while it may be correct grammatically, is misleading here. The awareness of being aware is totally void of individualizing psychic qualities. It is the condition of all consciousness rather than the differentiating "selfness" of a particular consciousness. If by "personal" we refer to the traits of a personality, I should say that this self-consciousness is individual but nonpersonal. It need not be empty of emotion. It may be a pain or a pleasure consciousness, for instance, but it is not accompanied by any sense of "I" or "me." It is pure intentionality, directed toward an object. One might be tempted to call it instantaneous, but that is not quite correct. All consciousness involves temporality for Sartre, for it is always directed toward a future and posited against the background of a past.

His insistence that the prereflective consciousness is egoless is heavily consequential for Sartre. By separating it from what is normally thought of as the personality, he postulates a radical freedom from psychological determinism as traditionally conceived. It is the prereflective consciousness which makes the original "choice of being," or fundamental project, by which we relate ourselves to the world. In *Being and Nothingness* Sartre argued that it is this nonpersonal self-consciousness that gives me my uneasy, usually unacknowledged realization that there is nothing absolutely fixed or necessary in this choice, that it might have been entirely different, and that it could—at least in theory— be replaced by another choice and consequently a different personality structure.

## (b) The Self as Ego

Another way to express this idea is to say that the familiar personal self is not part of the structure of a consciousness but its product. As a consciousness reflects back upon earlier acts of consciousness, it begins to impose a unity upon those experiences. The result is a network of interlocking responses in which the activity of an agent must always be assumed. The true agent, of course, has been the original prereflective consciousness, but as it is objectified by the reflective consciousness, it seems to take on qualities inseparable from the accumulation of particular interactions with the world. Here we have the emergence of the ego. We must not confuse this with the Freudian ego, which comprises only a part of the psychic structure. The Sartrean ego is coextensive with all of one's psyche; but note that psyche, for Sartre, refers to all of the mental and emotional *objects* of the reflective consciousness, not to the original prereflective consciousness. The ego, including both the "I" and the "me," is what most people mean by self in popular usage. In what we may call the natural attitude, it is made up of a bundle of character traits and a structured personality. It is what I *am*, manifested in a thousand external acts and reactions. The *I* both creates the *me* and springs forth from it so that, at least theoretically, I can study it in its now quiet past and therefore know the form it will take and how it will appear in the future. The ego is my permanent, enduring self, which distinguishes me forever from all other selves. Nevertheless, Sartre insists that the existence of the ego is purely ideal. It is the purely formal unity that a present consciousness perpetually imposes on its past and future intentional acts.

There is a difference according to whether it is the past or the future that we are considering. The essence of what I have been in the past is a part of my being—that being-in-itself which I (as being-for-itself) drag along behind my present existence—like a mermaid with her tail.[3] Thus it is correct, if rather pointless, to say that I have a self in the past, but the statement is true only from the point of view of the present. It is this self—the essential core of one's personal biography—which is the object of what Sartre calls "impure reflection." This last is ordinary introspection such as we frequently indulge in when we are recalling past happenings, trying to evaluate and to understand ourselves, to pin down our half-formed hopes and vague unhappiness. It is closely associated with the psychological analyses by novelists who seek to reveal to readers the complexity of emotional states. (Sartre alludes especially to Proust.) Impure reflection is a process of isolating and categorizing emotions, for example, as though they were things in themselves, and the whole procedure is carried out well within the framework of our fundamental project. Our psychic life, the object of our introspection, can indeed be grasped by a consciousness, however inadequately, either my own or that of therapist or biographer. Yet despite our familiarity with our autobiography, we recognize the sense of frustration that accompanies our attempt to pin down the real me or true self. The explanation lies in the fact that I apprehend an object where I sought to lay hands on a subjectivity. What is original about Sartre's rediscovery that the subject who thinks is not the subject thought of is precisely the fact that the original self-consciousness is not the personalized self. To ask what kind of self I am is to formulate the question improperly. Instead, I should ask what kind of self "my" consciousness has created.[4] This is indeed to raise more than a psychological question. Sartre has noted that it is on the level of *pure reflection* that morality is posited.[5] For a consciousness to look at its own product and to pass judgment on it is the original ethical act. But what is pure reflection? Is it an attainable goal or an illusion?

Sartre acknowledged that he had never adequately clarified his intention with regard to pure reflection. I think I know why. There is a troublesome ambiguity in the term itself. It hints at an ethics, and it suggests a form of self-knowledge. But Sartre states explicitly that consciousness cannot know itself knowing. If taken as a self-knowing, the ideal of reflection is impossible to achieve. For Sartre knowledge is consciousness' direct presence to an object in-itself. The self of prereflective consciousness cannot become the object of knowing at the same time that this consciousness is the reflecting agent. Perhaps it is easier to represent this in French than in English. We have seen that in every conscious act there are two things:

1. *conscience de l'objet*
2. *conscience (de) soi*

In reflective consciousness (assuming it to be a form of knowing) we would have the same situation.

1. *conscience de soi (= l'objet)*
2. *conscience (de) soi*

There is no way to suppress the second line. We attempt simply to combine these in a single line

*conscience de conscience (de) soi*

But this would be to suppress the self-awareness of the reflecting consciousness. It is equally impossible to perform the act which might be expressed as

*conscience (de) soi de conscience (de) soi.*

That is, we cannot do it if we intend that the second *conscience (de) soi* is the same as the first one. The intermediate *de*, which is the verbal equivalent of the act of nihilation that accompanies every intentional consciousness, separates them as surely as they are separated in their position on the page. We may say either that there is not enough separation between the two: the reflecting, since it *is* the reflected-on, cannot get outside it. Or we may say that there is too much separation: the object of consciousness is no longer the present consciousness but a past consciousness. The reflecting is no longer the same as the reflected. Sartre expresses the dilemma in a homely image. A donkey tries to reach a carrot attached to a stick fastened to the shaft of the cart he is pulling. Every movement to touch the carrot pushes it out of reach.[6] We cannot make of our consciousness an object without falling to the level of impure reflection.

Pure reflection, Sartre says, is not a full knowledge but rather a *recognition*; it is not a new consciousness but an internal modification of the prereflective consciousness. Sartre compares it to the situation of a person writing while aware that someone else is watching him. Indeed, pure reflection is the first faint hint of my having, factually, an outside, of my being-for-others. Even if alone, a consciousness can be, as it were, its own witness, but it can be so only if an external object is retained. In the midst of an activity I may suddenly reflect on myself as performing it without ceasing to keep the job to be done as the object of my consciousness. As I reflect, I am aware also that I am *not* the activity any more than I would be a tree that I observed. Joseph Catalano gives a particularly clear example taken from sport.

> If I am now reflecting on my playing tennis, I am aware of myself as playing tennis; I am certain that the self-that-is-playing tennis is the self reflecting on my tennis playing.... When I reflect on my tennis, I am aware that I can never perfectly *be* the self that is playing tennis. But this very nihilation (which is reflection), namely, that I can not-be a self that is identified with my tennis playing has its origin within the act of tennis playing, within the *being* of the original pre-reflective awareness that the being of consciousness is not identified with the being of tennis playing.[7]

Sartre himself chooses for illustration of the difference between prereflection and reflection Descartes' enterprise of doubting and points out that in "Cogito, ergo sum," the cogito is already on the reflective level.

Whether we consider the reflecting tennis player or the French philosopher seeking to prove his existence by trying to doubt it, we are immediately aware that reflection involves temporality. To be aware of myself doing something is to be aware of myself relating what has just been to what is to come. Pure reflection reveals to consciousness that as a nihilating intention, it is a pursuit of self, not a self that *is*.

It is easy to grasp that this over-the-shoulder glimpse of consciousness is possible, but why does Sartre assign to it so much importance? How can it possibly serve, as Sartre at the end of *Being and Nothingness* suggests that it might, as a basis for a new ethics?[8]

Where Sartre has not spoken, we cannot make assertions for him with any confidence, but I believe that he has given us a slight hint. Sartre recognized that it is possible to reflect on the memory of a nonreflective experience. I think we can see here the germ of one form of pure reflection — the attempt to hold up to consideration the elements and intrinsic qualities of the spontaneous conscious act, stripped of the overlay of associations after-the-event; the intent would be to examine a choice or an act as it was in itself at the time of its making. Precisely this is the aim of Hugo in *Dirty Hands*; but Hugo fails. Forced to rely on memory, he is unable to establish with certainty the reasons why he shot Hoederer in the past; he can only determine now the meaning he would like the act to have for the future. Granted that years had elapsed and Hugo had changed. But his failure perhaps explains why Sartre never developed the concept of pure reflection. Is it ever possible to be sure that one has isolated a former act of consciousness from its later overlay? Perhaps Sartre believed that we might train ourselves to look at our only-just-past reactions and to isolate what was genuinely spontaneous from what was influenced by individual and social presumptions. But this is to state a truism, or else Sartre envisioned some technique which he lacked the capacity, ability, or will to spell out. Sometimes I wonder if pure reflection is anything different from Sartre's habit of thinking against himself, of being willing to throw everything into question — both the existing structures of society and the furniture of one's psychic habitation. Sartre seemed to say as much in a late interview.

> You know, I have never described [pure reflection]. I said that it could exist, but I showed only the facts of accessory reflection. Subsequently I discovered that the non-accessory reflection was not a way of looking that was different from the immediate, accessory way of looking but was the critical work you can perform on yourself during a whole lifetime, through praxis.[9]

Sartre certainly suggests elsewhere, and perhaps implies even here, that the self which is the goal of pure reflection is indeed the original *con-*

*science (de) soi*, but the purpose of reflection would not be to discover that self as object but to liberate it from the incrustations of ego. This view would fit in with a remark by Sartre in *The Transcendence of the Ego*. There he says that in pure reflection the ego may be present but only "on the horizon" and as something which consciousness overflows and maintains by a continuous creation. He adds, "Perhaps the essential role of the ego is to hide from consciousness its own spontaneity."[10] The reason, of course, would be fear of what the full realization of our freedom would entail. Paradoxically, the revelation of the selfness of prereflective consciousness brings the realization that there is no self as substance, that a free consciousness has never been identical with the self it has made in the past or with the self that it projects toward the future.

## (c) The Self as Value

So far we have not discussed the future dimension. Sartre, we recall, claims that the ego is the ideal unity imposed by consciousness on all its psychic activity, future as well as past. Unlike the past, the future does not belong to being-in-itself. As the not yet, it depends on the nihilating action of the for-itself, which transcends what exists here and now. The future, so far as particular futures are concerned, has a purely virtual existence. There is no way to predict the dispositions and reactions of that "I" who will keep the rendezvous with the future that I presently project — not even if the world and other persons should perform their parts perfectly. The ego here is called on to unify acts still wholly imaginary. To speak of a future self is to postulate that a consciousness will continue to create a self that can be grasped only retrospectively. But Sartre now introduces an entirely different concept of self, one which does not belong to the ego and which is by definition never realized. Under the heading "The Self and the Circuit of Selfness," he discusses a self that is purely ideal, a value that we try to realize. It is metaphysical (or ontological) rather than psychological. We might think of our pursuit of this self as a corollary to the curtailed project of pure reflection.

Sartre argues that the for-itself is a lack of being which seeks to achieve being. Several other ways in which he expresses this idea might be formulated as follows: Consciousness is process, not substantial entity. It exists only as directed toward something other than itself. Consciousness is consciousness *of* something (Husserl). It is born, supported by a being which it is not (Sartre). Human reality is not what it is in the way that natural or manufactured things are. Human reality is what it is not and is not what it is. As a lack of being, the for-itself reaches out toward being. Consciousness is not a self and does not have a self; but as a self-making process, it pursues a self. Or, as Sartre says, it seeks to come to itself.

This future self Sartre links with desire and equates with value. He calls it a value because it is always the still unattained object of my desire. If I am thirsty, he says, what I desire is not just a glass of water but a thirst satisfied. I want to be simultaneously a desire as lack and a desire fulfilled, to be conscious of myself as a lack that is filled.[11] Thus the ultimate desire or value, of which all other desires are tributary expressions, is that I should *be* the self I have to make. This ideal is, of course, the desire to be in-itself-for-itself, which Sartre describes as the self-contradictory passion to be the Self-cause, or God.

Clearly one cannot have both unrestricted freedom to grow and a built-in program. If each consciousness is a continuous self-projection, we cannot say that the future self exists or will be grasped in the way that for the traveler the city of his destination exists and will eventually be reached by him. Yet we may raise the question as to whether pure reflection, in the extended sense in which we interpreted it with respect to the past, is relevant as regards our future consciousness. Obviously there can be no reflexive reaction on the future, but I think there is one way in which pure reflection can function so as to keep the future open to a free consciousness. The pure reflection which reveals to me that my spontaneous prereflective consciousness is not imprisoned within an ego can act to prevent me from preparing to make the future a repetition of the past, out of anxiety or insecurity. Frequently one rehearses so thoroughly the part one will play in a future event that one blinds oneself to unexpected possibilities and blocks off in advance any chance of spontaneous choice. A pure reflection not only would open up the past to new meaning but would regard the future as provisional.

At this stage we can see the wide variations in Sartre's use of the term "self," and we can recognize how distinctively and how precisely "self" must be employed in a Sartrean oriented psychotherapy. Obviously any notion of self as a two- or three-tiered structured psyche, such as Freud or Jung conceived, is out of the question. So is the humanistic concept of self-actualization if it is attached to a coherent pattern of inborn potentialities — what I like to call the "acorn theory" as presented, for example, in the work of Fromm and Maslow. The primary task for the person who would live in good faith (in Sartrean terms) is to keep the various categories of self clear in one's attitude toward one's life. This means, as Sartre puts it, that I should live with the realization that my nature is a demand but not a recourse. The ego is neither the cause of my actions nor a pattern to guide them; it is not a fixed self though it may be thought of as the self to which my consciousness has become accustomed. My spontaneous self-consciousness (the prereflective consciousness) is responsible for each new choice just as it has been the author of what I have made myself in the past.

## (d) The Self as Embodied Consciousness

Up until now I have been considering consciousness and psyche almost as if they were unembodied, but such was never Sartre's intention. In everyday experience my sense of my own self and of the Other's self is inextricably linked with the body even if, on some occasions, I may feel that there is a certain incongruity between external appearance and the inward life. It is natural for us to want to use the word "self" to refer to the total person even though Sartre tends to avoid this usage. In any case we cannot adequately grasp the sense in which Sartre's three kinds of "self" come into play unless we include the body. For a philosopher who has sometimes been mistaken for an idealist, the early Sartre assigned considerable importance to the body. In *The Emotions*, while he rejected the James-Lange theory which claimed that bodily reactions *caused* the emotions, Sartre nevertheless kept body on the active side; it is not a mere passive receptor or register of psychic reactions. Speaking of emotional behavior rather than of purely internal states (if indeed we may claim that these exist), Sartre claims that my consciousness assumes the emotional mode as a magical way of altering a lived situation in which I cannot modify the world itself. By effecting bodily changes, I alter my relation to the world. For example, I faint in the path of a menacing monster, thus "annihilating" myself since I cannot annihilate the beast. Or a woman patient is racked with uncontrollable sobbing *in order that* she may be unable to articulate a painful confession to the therapist.[12] In short, emotional behavior is purposeful and seeks to effect its purpose by means of the body. In *The Transcendence of the Ego* the body stands for "the illusory fulfillment of the I-concept" on the nonreflective level. It supports the empty, purely formal "I-concept" which allows me to answer, without intermediate mental process, the question, "What are you doing?" when my action has been nonreflective. If I am breaking up sticks,

> I say, 'I' am breaking up sticks, and I see and feel the object 'body' engaged in breaking the sticks. The body thus serves as a visible and tangible symbol for the *I*.[13]

*Being and Nothingness* has a long chapter devoted to the body. Sartre claims that we must recognize that it has three ontological dimensions: First, there is the Other's body—or the body for the Other. Here Sartre stresses the fact that I always consider the Other's body as the expression of a consciousness, not as an inert object in the world. Second, there is my-body-as-known-by-the-Other. At times the body (whether my own or the Other's) is pure object, as when I probe for a sliver or diagnose the extent of an injury. Of more concern to us here is the third dimension—the body-as-for-itself. This is the lived body or—as Sartre phrases it—the body I exist. Sartre denies any dualism. Sensations are not a hybrid something—not quite subjective, not quite objective—which are sent to consciousness by the body. The body *is* conscious. It is in and through the body that consciousness is present to the world, that it is individualized, that it has facticity, that it has a past. But consciousness does not use the body as an instrument for its separate needs. The relation is not that of agent and tool. A non-thetic awareness of body is inseparable from consciousness.

> The body is what this consciousness *is*; it is not even anything except body. The rest is nothingness and silence.[14]

The last half of the quotation reminds us that we cannot reduce consciousness to body. It is nothing except body, but we must read this in the sense that consciousness is no thing, that it is a nihilating process. As for-itself, the body is not the object *of* consciousness as it is in the other two dimensions. Consciousness does indeed nihilate the body in the way that Being-for-itself nihilates all Being-in-itself. But its nihilation of its own body is different from its nihilation of perceived objects in the world. The relation is closer to the bond that links present to past acts of consciousness. Mentally, as physically, the point of view of consciousness has the body as center of reference. If my eyes pain me as I read, my reading consciousness is also a pain-consciousness, and I do not separate the two, except in reflection, any more than I separate my view of a landscape from the conditions of light and air that enfold and reveal it.

The purely physiological aspects of body are virtually ignored in *Being and Nothingness*. When Sartre does mention them, he always adds that a free consciousness determines one's reactions. It is my basic choice of being that decides whether my fatigue enhances the pleasure of a hike or serves as an excuse for resting or turning back. Even under the sadist's knife, my consciousness decides when and whether I can no longer endure the torture. In the caress and embrace of sexual desire, the lover seeks to *incarnate* his own and the beloved's consciousness, in the vain hope of grasping the Other's entrapped consciousness as one skims the cream off milk. Moments of ultimate physical closeness (not the completion of orgasm) are supremely satisfying in realizing symbolically the impossible union in oneness of consciousnesses. What normally passes for a psychosomatic phenomenon was of no interest to Sartre at this date. It becomes of major importance in his study of Flaubert.

Let us turn now to *L'Idiot de la famille* and observe how Sartre uses the different notions of self when he attempts to understand the concrete reality of a once living person.

*L'Idiot de la famille*, a three-volume study of Flaubert which attempts to combine the approach of existential psychoanalysis with that of Marxist sociology, offers a final synthesis of Sartre's thought. As compared with his earlier books, the work shows no glaring theoretical inconsistency in its analysis of areas where Sartre or we would use the term "self," but the difference in emphasis and the added significance that are assigned to ego and body give us a much different picture of the interplay of subjective consciousness and conditioning and of how personality is developed. These nearly three thousand pages do not lend themselves to an easy summary of what Sartre believes to be "the truth of Flaubert." I will limit myself to a few observations which are especially relevant to the various uses of "self" by Sartre as I have outlined them.[15]

*(a) The Self of Prereflective Consciousness*

In the Flaubert study we find virtually no discussion of the free prereflective consciousness as such, but existence is everywhere implied. We see this partly by what is omitted. There is a total absence of any mention of genetic or endocrinological determinism. Sartre explicitly rejects the existence of innate genius or talent, and the idea of intelligence as something biologically given and measurable. Far from positing that Gustave Flaubert had any natural facility with words, Sartre argues that it was Gustave's difficulty with language which led him eventually to literature. He gives considerable weight to the psychosomatic, but the emphasis is always on the underlying intention. He insists that Flaubert's famous nervous crisis in 1844, which all biographers recognize as a turning point in his life, was due to hysteria, not epilepsy. Where Benjamin Bart, for example, sees Flaubert as a novelist whose will to succeed triumphed over the ravages of a disease which impaired his powers,[16] Sartre views the crisis as the neurotic but successful solution of an otherwise insoluble conflict. To Flaubert himself it seemed like a death and rebirth. It was in fact a self-effected liberation, won at great psychic cost.

Freedom has not been lost in *L'Idiot de la famille*, but it appears chiefly in the paradoxical form in which Sartre presented it in an interview at the time of the first publication of the work.

> A man can always make something out of what is made of him. This is the limit I would today accord to freedom: the small movement which makes of a totally conditioned social being someone who does not render back completely what his conditioning has given him.[17]

Sartre periodically directs our attention to the indispensable "small movement" amidst what would otherwise pass for a classic study of psychological determinism and unconscious conditioning. He does this partly by relying on his early concept of bad faith as a lie to oneself, in which the subject is never wholly ignorant of what he refuses to reflect or acknowledge. But now he attaches less of moral condemnation and speaks rather of the opaqueness of the lived experience (*le vécu*). A distinction between knowledge and comprehension, mentioned in *Being and Nothingness* but not fully developed, becomes crucial in the Flaubert study. A person may be wholly aware of an impulse, a wish, may vaguely sense its connection with an underlying structure of personal significances, without holding it up to a purifying reflection that would result in the kind of knowledge demanding deliberation and decision. What happens is something like what occurs more overtly when one looks at a set of papers piled helter skelter on the desk. One feels, "I ought to look over those. Some of those things certainly need attention. But I won't get into it now." Sartre claims that behavior such as "failure conduct" or the will to fail (*conduite d'échec*), is intentional (i.e., purposeful) but not deliberate. He notes that Flaubert himself referred to the "fulgurations" or sudden revelations of the stageset of his life world. One of these was expressed in the adolescent Gustave's unexpected realization that he envied, in a person he despised, the man's capacity for immense and genuine feeling. In later life a moment of retrospective self-understanding effected the confession to George Sand, "I was a coward in my youth."

Pervading the pages of *Being and Nothingness* was the presence of an anxious consciousness seeking in vain for meaningful structure outside itself and forced to recognize that rational order and purpose were only the thin human overlay imposed upon an incomprehensible world of matter. Flaubert himself was not disposed to recognize the terrifying responsibilities of this lonely freedom though he did in fact seek refuge in art from what he conceived to be the futility of existence in a world that failed to meet our high aspirations. We find a truly Sartrean echo of our despair in the face of an alien world, in one of his important digressions; somewhat surprisingly, the context is a discussion of practical jokes.

Sartre observes that it is through the world that I come to know myself. (Recall that all consciousness is consciousness *of* something other than itself.) "The world is what separates me from myself and announces me to myself" (II. 1312). Most of the time I exist with the assumption that things are indeed roughly what they seem. Despite my knowledge that my senses have on occasion deceived me, I cannot live without assuming that there is a broad area of daily life in which they can be trusted. Yet I retain a slight awareness of the ultimate unknowability in the things of which I am conscious. While the anguished awareness of this uncertainty is not present in every act, it exists as part of our "global feeling of our insertion in the world." What Sartre is speaking of is not just my realistic fear of accidents but a fundamental sense of estrangement. The practical joke is an attempt to evoke deliberately a rupture in the normal world of the person who is duped. Suppose that I, the victim, am offered what looks like a sugar cube for my tea but is actually a piece of celluloid. When it floats, I have a momentary but total feeling of disorientation. "I appear as a stranger to myself, my customs are disqualified, my past abolished, I am naked in a new present which is lost in an unknown future." Suddenly my secret suspicion is confirmed:

> My relation with being, with *my* being, was only an appearance; the *true* relation is discovered. It is horrible; I come to myself, a terrifying monster through a monstrous world. (II. 1313)

To be the dupe of one practical joke is unlikely to be fatal; it may even be salutary. A prolonged series of practical jokes perpetrated on the same victim, especially if it is a child, might well induce, Sartre suggests, "an artificial psychosis by forcing him to live his normal adaptation to the real as a permanent disadaptation"[18] (II. 1314).

### (b) The Self as Ego

This last statement by Sartre takes us away from the abstract, isolated consciousness confronting the world and others as objects and reminds us of the way that the Other as subject may intrude into the most private recesses of my relations with myself; that is, with my self in the sense of ego. In *L'Idiot de la famille* there are at least three important contexts in which Sartre uses his own distinctive concept of ego as the product of consciousness, not as the subject synonymous with consciousness. The first concerns what Sartre believes to be Gustave's nonverbalized belief with regard to his own ego and its formation. For reasons which we will note shortly, the child Gustave, Sartre claims, failed to develop as an active agent. Instead, he conceived of himself as being made by the Other. By means of other people's acts and words, he hoped to learn who he was. In short, his ego was an alter ego, both in his own mind and, to a degree, in reality. In Sartrean terms we may say that Gustave widened the breach between basic consciousness and the ego, feeling that his ego was the product not of his own consciousness but of others' and that there was no escape from it. Sartre finds evidence in Flaubert's adolescent writing that he felt that other people (his father especially) had made him what he was. At the same time he retained obscurely a resentful consciousness of being a free impulse which did not want to be limited to this nature that had been bestowed upon him.

Sartre appears to share this view. In his discussion of the gradual development of Flaubert's adult personality, he brings to bear all of the familiar elements of family conditioning—my second point. Gustave's "prehistory" includes the background and character of his parents, his relation to siblings (not only the older brother and younger sister who lived, but also the two brothers who died before he was born and the expected sister whose place he usurped.) "Protohistory" is Sartre's term for the early years of childhood. We may subdivide it into what he calls "constitution" and "personalization." Constitution refers to the fundamental patterns of affectivity which Sartre believes are set by the infant's relations with its mother. Personalization, beginning in protohistory but extending beyond it, refers to the way that the child internalizes and unifies its lived situation in the family. Although the mother's role is still important in personalization, Sartre gives primary emphasis, in the case of Gustave, to the influence of the father and less directly of the brother. We will look more specifically at the parental influences when we consider Sartre's treatment of psychosomatic factors in the fully embodied consciousness we know as Gustave Flaubert. For the moment I will simply point out that the discussion of Gustave's psychic formation, although it is superficially closer to a traditional psychoanalytical approach than one might have expected, remains distinctively Sartrean. Parental influences are fully as significant in Sartre's analysis as in Freud's, but they are handled differently. Though Sartre may refer to the Oedipus complex, for example, his discussion of the child's psychological development bears no relation to the patterned stages of sexual and personal evolvement as outlined for males and females respectively in psychoanalytical texts.

A third illustration of Sartre's use of his concept of the ego occurs when he is discussing reading. As one would expect in a work by Sartre on Flaubert, considerable weight is given to the effect on Gustave of the books he read. Sartre is interested in the nature of the literature itself, both as an expression of the social factors which produced it and as a molding influence on a new generation of writers. What is more relevant to us here is his discussion of just how we as readers empathize with an imaginary character and why fiction is so effective in helping to form a personality and even on occasion to alter our points of view. Sartre's explanation works only if we accept his basic position on consciousness and the psyche. Since the basic consciousness which I am is not structured, there is always implicit in me the awareness that my ego stands apart, at the horizon, as it were, of my consciousness, as the result of my structuring of experience. Therefore, since the ego is a quasi-object in the field of the reading consciousness, I as reader am free to project my ego into the ego of the character. As I identify my self with his, suddenly the reactions of the hero become part of my own past. As Sartre reminds us, our memory often confuses real events with imaginary ones. (We recall the way in which one's dream of a person may color one's attitude toward him or her in waking life.) I cannot move into the fictional world of another being without modifying the color of the world in which I live when I am not reading.

Something else happens, too, Sartre says, while I read empathetically. Although the "I" of my ego and the "I" of the hero are merged, I retain the feeling that each is inextricably linked with a transparent consciousness. Since the hero has been objectified by the author, I seem to grasp the hero's free consciousness — and my own — as objects even while I remain subject. Suppose that I am reading the tale of a Castilian nobleman. Sartre writes,

> The Castilian is [the reader] himself appearing to himself at last as the object which he is in the world, and at the same time the Castilian is his [the reader's] own subjectivity as it appears in *itself* to an impartial all-knowing observer. In short, it is the in-itself-for-itself finally achieved. (II. 1376)

The illusion depends in part also on the particular relation that exists between me and the author. It seems that out of the black marks on the page I freely create the fictional character and his world. But my creation is a re-creation in so far as it is guided by the inscribed intention of the author. One is inevitably reminded of Augustine's declaration — that our freedom consists in voluntarily doing God's will.

## (c) The Self as Value

Unexpectedly, we have moved from ego to the self as in-itself-for-itself, or value. It should not surprise us that this impossible goal is achieved only in an act of imagination. With respect to Flaubert and the ideal of self-coincidence, Sartre makes two important points. First, even as a child Flaubert thought of himself as living out a preordained destiny. As an adult he liked to think that he was incapable of change and inwardly impervious to anything which might touch him externally. He was what he was, once and for all. He refused, insofar as it was possible, to live with a future dimension. His life was a cyclic repetition. When political events transformed his society, he felt that he had outlived himself. And in fact critics have remarked that despite innovations in plot and setting, his last books have the same themes and attitudes as the early ones. Flaubert tried to defy time, not by remaining youthful in spirit but by considering himself already an old man when he was in his early twenties. Second, he chose art over life. Rather than to live as a man in time, he wanted to *be* the artist who creates imaginary eternities. He tried to make himself a work of art, partly by role playing, partly by casting himself in a form that excluded the transient and the spontaneous.

## (d) The Self as Embodied Consciousness

The somatic plays a major role in Sartre's analysis of Flaubert, both in the initial conditioning of his "constitution" or basic affectivity and in the climactic nervous crisis which established once and for all his "fundamental project"; that is, his way of being in the world. We observed earlier that Sartre attributes to the mother the primary responsibility for the baby's constitution. While denying that he himself has been influenced by Lacan, Sartre is like Lacan in stressing the symbiotic relation of the baby to its mother in infancy. Psychic and somatic are inextricably intertwined. Sartre claims that Madame Flaubert was overprotective but unloving in her treatment of the son who came when she wanted a daughter and whom in any case she did not expect to live very long.[19] Maternal love, Sartre declares, is not an emotion but a relation. The underloved child's first experience of himself as body is that of being a thing, dependent on another, but with no sense of reciprocity. The result in Gustave's case was a basic passivity fundamental to all of his reactions in later life.

On the sexual level, passivity and not a latent homosexuality or unresolved Oedipus complex was at the root of a certain femininity in Flaubert's character which his contemporaries noted. This hypothesis explains his intense, somewhat dependent relations with Louis Bouilhet and Maxime du Camp and his uneasy liaison with Louise Colet. Letters show that Flaubert was not impotent, but he appears to have feared Louise's strong sexuality as much as he longed for it. He saw her as seldom as he could manage, even at the height of his professed ardor. Like Léon in *Madame Bovary*, he seemed in some ways to be her mistress more than she was his. He expressed the wish that Louise could be man to the waist and woman below, that the two together might form, as it were, an hermaphroditic couple. What he really wanted, Sartre claims, was to be roused to virility by the caresses of the hands of the strong woman—in other words, the phallic mother.

Psychological consequents outside the sexual context were even more important. Nonvalorization was one of them, and Sartre claims that Flaubert never did develop the self-esteem that is requisite for being at ease with oneself. Sartre argues that the underloved child develops no sense of being an active agent in control of his destiny. To make the child feel that he is a sovereign around whom the world revolves, that it is he who decides what will happen, that the world awaits his striding down the path he will choose — all this is not to be regarded as the temptation of an overfond mother but rather the duty of an intelligent one. When we recall Sartre's view of the human being as a "useless passion," inhabiting a universe without support for human values, where nobody is privileged, we must conclude that Sartre is advising now the deliberate inculcation of a falsehood. But its intent is to instill in the child the true notion that he is an active agent who will make his own destiny (I. 143).

Sartre claims that the unloving overprotectiveness of Gustave's mother imprinted on the child's "constitution" (perhaps we would more naturally speak of "psychic disposition") a dependent passivity. There are still other consequences which Sartre obviously would expect to find in any child in a similar situation. First is a certain aboulia, a lack of capacity for true desire, which manifested itself even in Gustave's childhood as ennui or distaste for life. Sartre believes that if a baby is fed and cared for strictly by an adult's schedule with no concern for his specific hungers, thirsts, and discomforts, he fails to make the natural association between desiring and satisfaction and may never learn the pleasure of being satisfied. Then, too, helplessness creates a feeling of unreality. Sartre cites an episode from his own life and one from Gide's *Journal* to illustrate the way that one's sense of being totally out of control and at the mercy of external forces can leave one with the feeling that what goes on is not really happening, is like something in a dream (in dreams as we remember them, of course, not as we are immersed in them). Finally, Sartre adds, Flaubert's inability to feel clearly the distinction between real and unreal resulted in his confusing truth and belief — or better, in not recognizing the existence of truth as an absolute criterion. So strong was this feeling in Gustave that Sartre associates it with Flaubert's later decision to become a "worker in the imaginary," a creator of fiction. The mother's influence came first and laid the foundation for Gustave's passive constitution. Sartre speaks of this as "the first castration."[20]

The father not only reinforced the damage the mother had done, but exerted the decisive influence on Gustave's "personalization." Sartre dwells at length on the difficulties of a second son in the kind of patriarchal family in which the first boy plays the role of heir apparent. We have evidence for Gustave's jealousy of his older brother Achille. But Sartre goes far beyond the simple postulation of sibling rivalry. To be the younger son was to be marked as inferior, a pale copy or replica, at best a standby. Sartre thinks that there was a fatal interplay between Gustave's gradual realization of what it meant to be a second son and the natural difficulties inherent in moving from childhood to boyhood. Sartre speaks of the crisis of the "second weaning," which takes place when the child reaches the age of six or seven. This is the time when the engaging helplessness of the toddler is seen as clumsiness; the prattling cherub is suddenly a chattering nuisance. It marked the abrupt end of the "golden age" when Dr. Flaubert took Gustave along with him on his house calls. Gustave now is left at home, and his mother tells him that he must learn to read. Family documents record that Gustave had great difficulty in grasping the skill of reading, whereas Achille had mastered it easily. Sartre makes a great deal of this incident. He gives three reasons for Gustave's troubles. (We may observe once again the absence of physical explanations such as dyslexia or other natural disability.) First, he was suddenly called upon to act, but his constitutional passivity had not prepared him for the role of active agent. Second, he had regarded words as things which came from the Other. He had not learned reciprocity. It was not natural for him to reconstruct their meaning for himself. Finally, his presentiment of what would be demanded of him made him reluctant to leave the golden age of childhood. Gustave did indeed finally learn to read, but the crisis was catastrophic. Dr. Flaubert concluded that his son was retarded. Gustave accepted the pronouncement of his inferiority. It is from this episode that Sartre gets his title: *The Family Idiot.*

In the literary pieces which Flaubert wrote in his early and mid-adolescence, Sartre finds documents to support his picture of Gustave's life-world. The boy lived in an environment both theological and feudal. God the Father had justly condemned his evil son, but the prodigal longed and secretly hoped for forgiveness. The Father was a feudal suzerain who had no use for the homage of the vassal who loved him. The son exiled from Paradise simultaneously accepted the malediction and resented it. He loved his father and wished for his death. He resolved to live out his unhappy fate to its extreme in the hope that at last the cruel father would pity the son he had destroyed.

When Gustave went to school, his pride in being a Flaubert and his shame at being the rejected, inferior cadet resulted in two modes of behavior: compensating daydreams and aggressiveness. These were two sides of a coin. The fantasies were sado-masochistic. Sometimes Gustave imagined himself to be a Giant looking with scorn on the stupidity and baseness of the human ants below; often he identified himself with a cruel, destructive, powerful figure like Nero. In the schoolyard he was bitingly sarcastic in his taunts and not above joining with others in verbally tormenting the weak. He seems also to have been the leader in creating an imaginary character, the Garçon. Taking turns at the role, the boys used this fictional being as a mouthpiece by which to mock both bourgeois values and the dreams of the Romantics. Sartre claims that this spontaneous social psychodrama was therapeutic for the group and for Gustave but in quite different ways. For most of the boys it was effective in ridding them of the temporary aberrations induced by empathy with Romantic heroes — metaphysical despair and temptations to suicide. They became, like the Garçon, reconciled to enjoying the benefits of being bourgeois, even as they scoffed at its refined pretensions. Gustave enjoyed the double reward of being loved as one of the group and yet believing that he had demoralized his companions. To demoralize, Sartre insisted, remained Flaubert's chosen mission as a writer. *Madame Bovary*, for example, shows us that, except in art, there is no alternative to the foolish, self-defeating dreams of Emma and the gross materialism of the successful Homais.

In describing how Gustave finally came to grips with his family situation and by the same stroke launched himself on his career as an artist, Sartre ties together the constitutional passivity, paternal conditioning, and the psychosomatic. At the lycée Gustave's record was respectable but not brilliant. When he excelled, it was in those fields least propitious for a prospective medical student — in history and literature. Rather than explaining this record as the result of natural interests or talents, Sartre sees it resulting from Gustave's resolve not to imitate Achille but to demonstrate the inferiority to which his father had condemned him. This was the first manifestation of what Sartre calls "failure conduct" or, to use the more familiar term, the will to fail. It is an obvious strategy to be employed by a "passive agent." The latter is Sartre's term for one whose constitution is marked by passivity. When he acts, as all of us must do, willy-nilly, he tries to convince himself that he is coasting with the current, giving in to circumstances beyond his control, refusing to acknowledge his own part in shaping the circumstances.

A bourgeois son was expected to work at some sort of profession. Since Gustave showed no talent for medicine, the obvious alternative was law. He hated the very thought of it, but he was duly enrolled and even made a show of studying. Sartre describes him caught between two impossible demands: His passivity makes him incapable of defying his father, but he is equally unable to obey his father. To do so would be to sentence himself to a life in which he must not only acknowledge his mediocrity but seem to be contented with it. The sole solution is to show that he *cannot* obey. This means that he must accept total disgrace. He does in fact fail his first set of exams. But this is not enough. He will be expected to repeat them. Somehow he must demonstrate his inability to hold any kind of job. Now the negative strategy becomes a positive calculation. If he can stay at home, like an unmarried daughter, supported by his father until eventually he inherits his share of the estate, then he will have everything he requires. The dependent, feminine aspect of his personality will be fostered. He, and not the brilliant Achille, will live in the bosom of the family, who will be forced to pity him, to care for him, hence to love him. And he will be free to write. Radical failure will be a form of salvation. Loser will win.

It would have been easy for Sartre to defend such a hypothesis if he had been willing to resort to the concept of an unconscious. Sartre tries to work without it. The will to fail, he says, can be sustained only as a project in bad faith. But a divided intention, auto-suggestion, and somatic reactions are essential accompanying elements. The conflict was genuine and manifested itself on at least three levels. First, Gustave's fear of public failure and parental displeasure was acute, as painful in immediate anticipation as was the more remote hated career. Either outcome was intolerable. Second, Gustave at times tried to assume the role of active agent. He declared to a friend his resolve to work disdainfully until he had won his law degree and then refuse to practice. But the habit of passive obedience was so strong in him that he must have known that this was sheer bravado. If defiance were to be his solution, now was the time to announce it. Finally, two attitudes, deriving respectively from the family's attitude and from his reading in Romantic literature, were mutually contradictory: the Flaubert pride demanded that the greatest must show himself able to do the least. But opposed to this was the ideal of the Romantic hero whose greater vision prevented him from seeing how to perform the lowly task at his feet—the eagle that loses the footrace, or Plato's philosopher newly descended into the cave. Each set of attitudes poisoned the other. Gustave would in all sincerity force himself to study and try to succeed—as indeed he did on his retake of the first examinations. But most of the time his efforts were self-defeating. He would postpone study until the last moment; then in a sudden panic he would try to do too much in too short a time. Having decided in advance that the legal code was meaningless jargon, he attempted to master it by sheer memorization, refusing to take the intellectual steps which, by viewing law as the evolutionary accretion of historical development or as logical construction, might have made it interesting and easier to retain. He neglected his physical well-being so that ill health by itself might render him incapable. Finally, as it became obvious that only a desperate solution would save him, he called on his body for more decisive intervention.

Sartre cites several pieces of evidence to show that Flaubert, however confusedly and inaccurately, was aware of the interaction of psychic and bodily reactions. Gustave applied to himself the theory that in some persons agitations of the senses, instead of stimulating intellectual or artistic creativity, passed into the nervous system, causing physiological disturbances. This is what happens, he said, in the case of those musically talented children who will never be Mozarts. A second indication that Sartre finds is Flaubert's reference to a prolonged period of sexual abstinence at just this date. Combined with his confession to a sudden impulse toward self-castration which came over him one day, Sartre argues that probably Gustave found himself impotent in this time of pressure, not an unlikely thing to have happened. But Sartre goes on to hypothesize that Gustave associated the wish and the reality. Had a momentary, rejected impulse been accepted and acted on by the body? A third point refers to earlier days at home. Gustave had amused himself and the family by doing imitations of an epileptic, a former journalist who had been reduced to beggary by his affliction. Gustave recorded that he threw himself into this performance to the point of almost being in the other man's skin and added that his father, fearing it might have some harmful effect on his son, forbade any repetition of the act. Sartre claims that Flaubert was afraid lest his imitations of madness and his habit of imagining abnormal mental states might, through the power of suggestion, induce his body to succumb to insanity.

If we follow Sartre, Gustave during the months preceding January 1844 awaited something decisive that would come to him from outside — the quintessence of "active passivity." Certainly the timing of his nervous crisis suggests "intentional" hysteria and not a purely accidental epilepsy. After failing the second set of examinations, he had gone home for the winter holidays. If nothing happened to save him, he would have to return to the law books and try again. One night as he was driving with his brother a cart suddenly appeared out of the darkness, not colliding with the Flaubert vehicle but coming close. As though it were a sign, Gustave fell rigid to the floor. He did not lose consciousness but suffered severe pains, hallucinatory perceptions of strange lights, etc. During the subsequent weeks attacks returned, accompanied now by convulsions, but Flaubert appeared strangely relaxed and without anxiety. It was as though the worst had happened and there was nothing more to fear. Was this simply because he had consented to the ignominy of failure and disgrace and now, having paid the price, could look forward to reaping the reward? Or was it also, as Sartre suggests, relief that he had risked death and insanity but had avoided them? Dr. Flaubert died a little more than two years later, in 1846. Soon afterward, and despite the fact that his beloved sister had died in childbirth shortly before the father's demise, Gustave declared that at last he could get to work at writing again. The attacks diminished in frequency and finally, after ten years, ceased entirely.

Sartre is speaking of hysteria, of course, not playacting and knowing deception. Obviously the nervous crisis was not the effect of a rational act of will any more than Gustave's failure to pass the examinations was due to feigned ignorance. Yet Sartre insists that Flaubert had a certain comprehension of the intentional structure behind the crisis. This is implied in his many references to his having sacrificed everything for art, to his having renounced all real passions in order to be able to depict them in art. His language constantly suggests that some sort of bargain had been made. When the last years of his life were disturbed by financial worries, he regarded it not merely as unfortunate but unjust. His laments sound like complaints over a broken contract. Finally, at Flaubert's great moment of disillusion, there was another psychosomatic occurrence. The fall of the Second Empire and the Prussian invasion of France were cataclysmic for Flaubert, who looked on the defeat of France as the end of Latin culture. In retrospect he felt that the Court of Napoleon III, in whose circles he had been lionized, had all been a sham, like a staged court in an opera. Science had triumphed over art. Imagination, instead of creating a higher reality, had helped to insure the real humiliation of the German occupation of Flaubert's own home at Croisset. Sartre states that at this date Flaubert found his whole life called into question and felt that after all loser had been self-deluded in thinking he had won. Statements in Flaubert's letters testify to his acute sense of having outlived himself. In his anger at his fellow citizens he wrote, "I would like to drown humanity in my vomit" (III. 496). Significantly, it was at this time that he was afflicted with spells of nausea so severe that he was convinced that he had developed a stomach ulcer. He consulted a physician, who could find no organic cause. Gradually the symptoms disappeared. Sartre explains the imagined ulcer as the expression of Flaubert's wish that he could vomit up himself because of his guilt at having enjoyed and been an accomplice of the regime responsible for today's dust and ashes. He rejected both the fossil he saw himself becoming and the deluded man who had not foreseen the outcome. As Sartre expresses it, Flaubert could only wait for death since he had lived beyond the period for which he had programmed himself.

### III

Who was Flaubert? Some critics of Sartre's biography of him have claimed that the study of conditioning has been carried to such an extreme that "Gustave" has been lost, that we are left with the feeling that any younger son in that family—or even a changeling—would have become the author of *Madame Bovary*. I hope I have shown, even by my few examples, that this is to misread Sartre, that Gustave as a passive agent still directed the course of his life. Sartre has remarked that Flaubert was at least free to choose to become the novelist we know, or a poor physician, or nothing but a typical bourgeois.[21] I would add that there are a number of places in the book at which one feels that his preference for the imaginary might also have induced him to choose psychosis.

# SARTRE'S CONCEPT OF THE SELF

John Weightman charged Sartre with a deficiency in his theory. In Weightman's view, Sartre's early rejection of "human nature" as a psychological given led him to miss "the physiological uniqueness, the given genetic identity of the individual Gustave." Weightman asks,

> If there is no density of the given individual nature, if there is no weighting to be derived from the various possibilities within the temperament, how can anyone get the inner leverage necessary for the exercise of freedom? Freedom cannot be rootless; it must be the margin of uncertainty in the possibilities of the given.[22]

The last sentence we may dismiss with the observation that Sartre himself might have written it; but for him the margin of uncertainty would be located at the moment of internalization of the given, and the given would refer to the subject's situation, not to genetic coding. The rest of Weightman's accusation reveals an inability to grasp — or else an unwillingness to accept — the distinction between consciousness and ego. Like most people in our Western tradition, he is unable to conceive of life as a true self-making and wants to see it as an unfolding. The differences between a rolling snowball and a Roman candle! The free consciousness that made Flaubert continued to manifest itself through layers of personal ego which it itself laid down and within the structures of the life world it had formed out of its environment.

If to the question, "Who was Flaubert?" we were to reply, "He was himself," the statement is correct or incorrect, in Sartrean terms, according to which use of self we have in mind. I like to think that there are two forms of self-realization consistent with Sartre's psychology.[23] The first is spontaneous self-realization and is based on my recognition that the core of my existence is inextricably bound up with nonbeing, the "nothingness" of which Sartre speaks, the separation between consciousness and all its objects (physical and mental) — my freedom itself. I need not (indeed *cannot*), in any absolute sense, *be anything*, but I am free to project being whatever I choose. I am separated from my past, from my future, even from my self (as fully personalized ego). Spontaneous self-realization is the realization of the power and the independence of the preflective consciousness.[24] In contrast, temporal self-realization depends on my acknowledging my responsibility for my own past and future; it necessitates that I relate them to the present in some coherent pattern. By my actions, Sartre tells us, I carve out my being — in the world; the image of what I have made myself is formed by the marks I have left on the total environment in which I have moved. What I am is what I have done — at this moment. "You are your life," Inez tells Garcin in *No Exit*. Obviously both kinds of self-realization are essential for full development of our freedom and responsibility. Spontaneous self-realization by itself results in the weather-vane personality, the irresponsible and finally valueless life. But to live wholly within the framework of one's chosen value system, even if once it was freely created, is to become "uptight," resistant to growth, incapable of enjoying the psychic refreshment of the "moral holidays" which, William James once said, are essential to our psychological well-being.

Sartre claims that Flaubert, insofar as he was able, refused spontaneous self-realization and chose to identify himself first with the ego "given" to him and then with his own carefully shaped self-image as artist. In reality both of these and the person history knows as Gustave Flaubert were the product of the original, nonpersonalized, prereflective self-consciousness, which neither Flaubert nor we could ever grasp and objectify.

## NOTES

1 *L'Idiot de la famille: Gustave Flaubert de 1821 à 1857* (Paris: Gallimard, Vols. I and II, 1971; Vol. I, 1972), p. 7. All translations in this paper are my own. Part One of this work has been published in English. *The Family Idiot*, translated by Carol Cosman (University of Chicago Press, 1981).

2 "Conscience de soi et connaissance de soi," *Bulletin de la Société Française*, Vol. XLII, No. 3, April-June, 1948, p. 69. Sartre's example is *il se penche*, which literally means to lean but may also be used in the sense of "to take an interest in." My example seems to me to be clearer for English-speaking readers. In this discussion Sartre defends and explains in more detail the view of consciousness which he presented in the first part of *Being and Nothingness*. It has been published in English as "Consciousness of Self and Knowledge of Self," translated by Mary Ellen and N. Lawrence, in *Readings in Existential Phenomenology*, edited by Nathaniel Lawrence and Daniel O'Connor. (Englewood Cliffs, New Jersey: Prentice Hall, Inc., 1967), pp. 113-42.

3 This is Sartre's image. *Being and Nothingness*, translated by Hazel E. Barnes (New York: Washington Square Press, 1972), p. 208.

4 Strictly speaking, the prereflective consciousness should not be qualified by personal pronouns, but I follow Sartre's custom in using them as we do in ordinary speech.

5 "Conscience de soi et connaissance de soi," p. 90.

6 *Being and Nothingness*, pp. 277-78. To be exact, Sartre's analogy refers to an attempt on the part of consciousness to escape from its own perpetual flight by making itself a fixed presence to the world. The image applies equally well in the context of my discussion.

7 Joseph S. Catalano, *A Commentary on Jean-Paul Sartre's* Being and Nothingness, (University of Chicago Press, 1980), p. 129.

8 In *Being and Nothingness* Sartre's discussion of pure reflection (pp. 211-21) does not mention any ethical implications. In the last paragraph of the book Sartre says that the ethical questions which he has just raised "refer to a pure and not an accessory reflection."

9 "Un Entretien avec Jean-Paul Sartre," with Michel Contat and Michel Rybalka. *Le Monde*, May 14, 1971. The interview has been published in English as "On the Idiot of the Family," translated by Paul Auster and Lydia Davis. In *Life/Situations* (New York: Pantheon Books, 1975), pp. 109-32.

10 "La Transcendance de l'Ego: Esquisse d'une description phénoménologique," *Recherches philosophiques*, Vol. VI (1936-37), p. 120. This has been published in English as *The Transcendence of the Ego: An Existentialist Theory of Consciousness*, translated by Forrest Williams and Robert Kirtpatrick (New York: Noonday Press, 1957).

11 On the surface Sartre seems to be simply wrong. The pleasure of drinking when one is thirsty is precisely one's awareness of desire in the process of being satisfied. Sartre appears to join in with Schopenhauer's gloomy appraisal of life as alternating between deprivation and satiety. Of course, Plato's more philosophical argument (in the *Symposium*) is relevant, too: that what love-as-lack desires is the continued (i.e., future) possession of the good and the beautiful; hence desire as such remains a deprivation or reaching toward that is not now possessed.

12 These are Sartre's examples. *The Emotions: Outline of a Theory*, translated by Bernard Frechtman (New York: Philosophical Library, 1948), pp. 62 and 31.

13 "La Transcendance de l'Ego," p. 115.

14 *Being and Nothingness*, p. 434. I have not listed the three dimensions in the same order as Sartre discusses them.

15 In this article I am not raising the question of the validity of Sartre's assertions concerning Flaubert so far as historical accuracy is concerned. I have discussed at length his interpretation of Flaubert in my book *Sartre and Flaubert* (University of Chicago Press, 1981). In referring to *L'Idiot de la famille* in this section, I will simply cite volume and page numbers.

16 Benjamin F. Bart, *Flaubert* (Syracuse: Syracuse University Press, 1967), pp. 93-7 and 752-53.

17 "Itinerary of a Thought," *New Left Review*, 58 (November-December, 1969), p. 45.

18 Sartre says that the motive of the prankster is to reassure himself. He himself knows that all is within the bounds of normality even when things seem in utter disarray to the victim. "This momentary mini-scandal appears, therefore, to be a vaccine against the anguish of existing." Still, adds Sartre, the joker is an anxious type. (II. 1314)

19 Sartre admits that we have no evidence for the nature of the relation between Madame Flaubert and the infant Gustave but offers it as a hypothesis which fits what we do know of her background and personality as well as of Flaubert himself.

20 Sartre speaks of a "second castration," which was Dr. Flaubert's refusal to recognize his son's early aspirations to be an actor. I think Sartre has been guilty of exaggeration, if not actual distortion, at this point. The matter is discussed in my book, mentioned above.

21 *Sartre, un film réalisé par Alexandre Astruc et Michel Contat* (Paris: Gallimard, 1977), p. 76.

22 John Weightman, "Battle of the Century—Sartre *vs.* Flaubert," *New York Review of Books*, April 6, 1972.

23 I have discussed the two kinds of self-realization more fully in my book, *An Existentialist Ethics* (Chicago: University of Chicago Press, 1978).

24 I mean, of course, independence of psychological determination or inner necessity. Consciousness is always dependent on its objects in that it cannot exist without an object.

# "Sense and Sensibility": Sartre's Theory of the Emotions

SANDER H. LEE

Jean-Paul Sartre, in his theory of the emotions, seems to offer as stark a contrast between the emotions and rationality as does Jane Austen in her famous novel. However, while Austen is usually viewed as making this distinction in a classical Aristotelian manner, Sartre claims to be offering us a description based on the combined applications of a "regressive phenomenological psychology" and a "progressive pure phenomenology." Some critics, however, have suggested that Sartre has done nothing more than simply perpetuated the rationalist position of Descartes, a position which sharply distinguishes between rationality and "the passions of the soul."

In this article, I would like to both clarify and critically examine Sartre's theory. I will begin by explicating what I consider to be the major features of this theory. In section two, I will present some criticisms of Sartre's description. In section three, I will present the Sartrian response to these criticisms. I will go on to examine this response in order to reveal the ontological basis for Sartre's attitude towards the traditional psychological approach to this issue. Finally, in section four, I will attempt to place Sartre's theory in the context of traditional theories of the emotions. I will conclude by suggesting the outline of a more fundamental criticism of Sartre's theory.

I will base my discussion on the theory Sartre gives us in his early work *The Emotions: Outline of a Theory* and on relevant passages from *Being and Nothingness*. I am aware that some of Sartre's perspective in the former is overly indebted to the writings of Husserl and Heidegger, yet it seems to me that a distinctively Sartrian theory is expressed in the work; one which can be discussed without reference to those Husserlian and Heideggerian notions which are used in the work but which Sartre later rejects.[1] I also believe that this early theory is fully consistent with the views he expresses in his later work.

I

Sartre describes emotional consciousness as an unreflective way of apprehending the world. Like all consciousness for Sartre, emotional consciousness is intentional, it is a consciousness whose object is rooted in the world. However, unlike reflective consciousness "in which the for-itself (consciousness) *is* in order to be to itself what it is,"[2] unreflective consciousness is spontaneous and non-thetical. Unreflective con-

67

sciousness is not unconsciousness (a state whose existence Sartre denies), but is a way of acting in which one is not conscious of acting at all.

This unreflective behavior is entered into, according to Sartre, in order to transform the world out of seemingly irresolvable difficulty into a realm of "magical" facility. In other words, when the usual methods for resolving problems are seen as being too difficult to apply, or when it appears to consciousness that no method at all exists which can be practically utilized to resolve difficulties, consciousness unreflectively chooses to radically transform its view of the world to one in which magic is the reigning force.

In such situations, consciousness denies the rational, reflective view of the world as controlled by deterministic processes which can be altered through the manipulation of instruments or tools, in order to enter a realm where consciousness truly believes that the world can be altered simply through the overwhelming desire to have it altered. Sartre gives many examples of this process. A hunter is charged by a raging lion, to which attack he responds by fainting. Here the hunter is faced with a situation in which there appears reflectively to be no escape. The hunter thus chooses to magically transform the world into a realm in which danger can be avoided by eliminating consciousness of that danger. This process Sartre refers to as passive fear.

Fear can also be active. Should the hunter drop his gun and start running away from the lion, he would be engaging in an active denial of the reality of the danger in which he finds himself, a danger he is unwilling to accept.[3] In another example, a man strains to reach some grapes hanging overhead. When he realizes the practical difficulty of reaching the grapes cannot be resolved, he responds by muttering, "They were too green."[4] Here the man resolves the tension which ensues from his inability to achieve his goal by projecting onto the world the inadequacy which he feels within himself.

Similar treatments are given to discussions of sadness and joy. Sadness results from an unreflective spontaneous choice to deny the reality of a situation in order to retreat either into a realm where the object of sorrow is denied ("My God, I can't believe she's dead!") or into a realm where consciousness denies the possibility of constructively facing its new circumstances ("I just can't go on without her."). Joy, on the other hand, is a magical attempt to instantaneously possess the totality of what one desires, rather than engaging in the prudent, often difficult process which would actually bring about such possession. A woman tells a man that she loves him and he responds by singing and dancing for joy, rather than engaging in "the difficult behavior which he would have to practise to deserve this love and make it grow, to realize slowly and through a thousand little details (smiles, little acts of attentiveness, etc.)

that he possesses it."[5] The man grants himself a respite from the prudent endeavor of seeking to achieve his goal in order to symbolically act out that achievement by way of incantations and gyrations.

Now Sartre does admit that there are such things as false emotions, feinted role-playing which one occasionally engages in at socially appropriate times. One might pretend to be sad at the funeral of a relative one disliked, or one might feint pleasure at the reception of an unwanted gift. However, Sartre's theory is a theory of genuine emotion, which only is present when consciousness truly believes in and freely chooses to enter into the magic realm. Once one chooses to initiate an emotional response, it is often very difficult, if not impossible, to disengage oneself from that emotion until it has run its course. The process of undergoing an emotion is a physical one which should be taken seriously as a commitment from which consciousness cannot easily retreat.

In this sense, emotion is a "phenomenon of belief."[6] Consciousness *lives* in the new world it has created through the mediating presence of the body.[7] Emotional consciousness is analogous for Sartre to sleeping consciousness in that both modes of consciousness create new worlds in which the body is transformed in such a way so that consciousness can experience these new worlds through "synthetic totalities."

Thus, concludes Sartre, "the origin of emotion is a spontaneous and lived degradation of consciousness in the face of the world."[8] Emotional consciousness is not aware of itself as a degradation of consciousness, "it has only a positional consciousness of the degradation of the world which takes place on a magical level."[9] Emotional consciousness is its own captive, it is absorbed in itself and it tends to be self-perpetuating. The more emotional one becomes, the more emotional one is likely to become. Such an escalating emotional cycle can only be broken either through a purifying reflection or through removal of the affecting situation. Only by such means can consciousness be released and returned to freedom.[10]

Admittedly, Sartre states, the world does sometimes appear as itself magical rather than determined. An earthquake, a solar eclipse, an erupting volcano can all be viewed as introducing magical qualities into the appearance of the world; however, if consciousness chooses to accept the magical interpretation of such events, it does so at the expense of reflective consciousness which is capable of interpretating such phenomena in a non-emotional context.

Finally, Sartre points out that pure reflective consciousness can direct itself to emotion by way of a phenomenological reduction which reveals consciousness in the process of constituting the world in terms of a magical realm. Through such a reduction one can come to realize that "I find it hateful *because* I am angry," rather than believing that "I am angry because it is hateful."[11]

## II

In casting a critical eye towards Sartre's theory, which I have now briefly summarized, one cannot help being struck by the pejorative view which Sartre takes towards the emotions. When we unreflectively choose to magically transform the world, we are choosing to engage in a behavior which "is not on the same plane as other behaviors; it is not *effective....* In short, in emotion it is the body which, directed by consciousness, changes its relations with the world in order that the world may change its qualities. If emotion is a joke, it is a joke we believe in."[12]

The emotional consciousness, therefore, is incapable of reaching its goals; it is an ineffectual way of dealing with the world. It is no more than a bad joke which consciousness unreflectively plays upon itself. Furthermore, as we have noted, emotional consciousness is a *degradation* of consciousness in the face of the world.

Well, ought we to accept such a disparaging description of the emotions? Is there not evidence both in our everyday experience and in Sartre's own ontology to suggest that perhaps such a description is not fully justified? I think these are questions which do deserve our attention.

To begin with, let us look at this issue of the potential effectiveness of emotional consciousness in gaining the ends which reflective consciousness chooses for itself. Returning to the example of the man who has just been told he is loved, one must question the accuracy here of Sartre's description. In choosing to react to this news by spontaneously dancing and singing for joy, Sartre suggests that this man is retreating from his purpose of possessing the love of the woman. He even suggests that the man is temporarily "abandoning" the woman.

However, is there not a much more plausible way to interpret such a scene? In choosing to dance and sing for joy, it seems to me that the man is not running away from his project of enjoying the love of the woman, he is *living* it. To express emotional satisfaction in the face of the world is not a denial of the world, it is an acceptance of it, an acceptance that is often extremely effective in helping us to gain our goals. We can easily imagine that the man's display of joy in the face of the woman's admission of love will only serve to further endear him in the eyes of the woman. Will not the woman be lead simply to love him all the more in response to the joy that he shows in her company?[13]

Furthermore, does not Sartre's interpretation of this scene reveal an even deeper misunderstanding of the role of the emotions in human life? For, it seems to me, Sartre is ignoring the fact that the man's goal in this scene is exclusively an emotional one. The aim of the man is to genuinely experience the emotion of love. Sartre himself makes it quite clear that his theory is one of genuine emotion, not of the kind of pseudo-emotion which might lead a man to seek a woman's love in a calculated attempt to fulfill some other goal. Yet, Sartre speaks as though this man can only be effective in achieving his goal if he discards the emotional consciousness and chooses to reflectively attempt to win the woman's heart in an emotionless calculating fashion.

But, to act in this way would be a negation of the man's entire project. Emotional aims can *only* be achieved through a choice to engage in and live the emotional consciousness. It would seem that the greatest weakness of Sartre's theory is his failure to realize that a great many of the goals consciousness set for itself are in fact emotional ones which can only be achieved in this fashion. He speaks as though the only goals consciousness sets for itself are pragmatic ones having to do with bringing about transformations in the structure of the world through the utilization of instrumental techniques which are in accordance with the deterministic processes of the world. To the extent that this is the case it is clear that emotional consciousness is not as effective as reflective consciousness in bringing about such changes.

If one has a flat tire on a lonely highway late at night, it is clear that swearing and kicking at the tire in anger is not as effective as pursuing an orderly and calm procedure of changing the tire. However, such non-emotional projects are not the only ones in which people engage. In fact, our experience suggests that people put a great deal more energy and even tend to put more value on the achievement of emotional rather than non-emotional goals. In many people's lives, the search for love predominates over all other enterprises. The emotional desire for friendships, affection, or even power often sets the direction in which we choose to live our lives.

Furthermore, the choice to enter the emotional consciousness is often very effective in achieving the goals of consciousness. If you regularly act in a way which irritates and disturbs me, I might very well achieve my goal of having you cease such behavior by getting openly angry with you and expressing that anger in such a way as to dissuade you from engaging in such behavior in the future. Indeed, such emotional behavior on my part might be much more effective in achieving my aim than would be a calm reflective attempt on my part to persuade you to change your habits. The expression of emotional vehemence often has much greater impact on others than does an emotionless response.[14]

### III

What we have revealed in the preceding section, it seems to me, is Sartre's disdain for the goals of the unreflective emotional consciousness. What we must now examine is Sartre's ontological basis for such disdain.

Why is the emotional consciousness a "degradation of consciousness"? This is a question I believe we can answer by examining Sartre's description of consciousness as it is presented in *Being and Nothingness*. In that work, Sartre again makes his distinction between reflective and non-reflective consciousness. Non-reflective consciousness, also called the "prereflexive Cogito" by Sartre, is direct consciousness of the world, immediate and spontaneous.

Reflection, on the other hand, involves the attempt on the part of consciousness to become its own object. Furthermore, Sartre distinguishes between two sorts of reflection, pure and impure (or accessory) reflection. "Pure reflection, the simple presence of the reflective for-itself (consciousness) to the for-self reflected-on, is at once the original form of reflection and its ideal form; it is that on whose foundation impure reflection appears, it is also that which is never first *given*; and it is that which must be won by a sort of catharsis."[15]

"But impure reflection, which is the first spontaneous...reflective movement is-in-order-to be the reflected-on as in-itself (the world)."[16] In other words, in impure reflection consciousness objectifies its emotional experiences in the form of psychic states which are viewed by consciousness as objective objects upon which consciousness may reflect. The spontaneous and on-going process of becoming in emotional experience is denied in an attempt to pretend that emotional experience can accurately be described in terms usually only used in connection with descriptions of the world external to ourselves (the in-itself).

Impure reflection is the type of methodology of which Sartre accuses traditional psychology of attempting to utilize in order to accurately delineate emotional consciousness. It is a methodology which is doomed to failure in that "it is an attempt to draw us towards a mechanistic interpretation of the psychic which, without being any more intelligible, would completely distort its nature."[17] According to Sartre, "it is necessary to give up trying to reduce the irrational element in psychic causality. This causality is a degradation of the ecstatic for-itself, which is its own being at a distance from itself, its degradation into magic, into an in-itself which is what it is at its own place. Magic action through influence at a distance is the necessary result of this relaxation of the bounds of being. The psychologist must describe these irrational bonds and take them as an original given of the psychic world."[18]

There are two points to be made here on the basis of Sartre's discussion of impure reflection. The first has to do with impure reflection as a method for describing emotional consciousness. Sartre claims (and I do not disagree with him on this issue) that impure reflection is an ineffectual and even a distorted way of regarding emotional consciousness, in that it reduces emotions to objectified states rather than revealing them as the subjective, irrational processes which we actually do experience. To this extent, psychologists who engage in impure reflection are acting in "bad faith" in that they are denying actual conscious experience in an attempt to lie to themselves as to the nature of the emotional consciousness as spontaneous and on-going through time.[19]

The second point brings us back to the original question raised in this section. What is Sartre's ontological basis for claiming that emotional consciousness is a degradation of consciousness? Well, we have now seen that the proper method for describing emotional consciousness is pure reflection, which reflects upon itself through a "nihilating" consciousness of it-self as a three-dimensional temporal process.[20] This is the method which Sartre claims to have at least partially used in his earlier work on the emotions. However, Sartre admits in that work that further investigation is required in order to more fully describe emotional consciousness. He states in his conclusion that his essay is only an "example" of the way in which such a methodology can be used in conjunction with a regressive phenomenological psychology in order to describe emotional consciousness.[21]

What I wish to maintain is that we can extend Sartre's pure reflection on emotional consciousness as described both in his earlier essay and in sections of *Being and Nothingness* in order to briefly summarize his ontological basis for claiming emotional consciousness is a degradation of consciousness. It seems quite clear from the quotes given above on the issue of impure reflection that Sartre views emotional consciousness as a degradation of consciousness away from it-self into a magical experience which is "at a distance from itself."[22]

In other words, emotional consciousness, *not* impure reflection, but *spontaneous emotional consciousness* is itself in bad faith. When consciousness unreflectively chooses to attempt to magically transform the world, it is attempting to deny just what it is; it is attempting to pretend that consciousness is not capable of pure reflection. When the man who fails to reach the grapes angrily mutters to himself that "they were too green, anyhow," he is attempting to lie to himself, to escape his own condition as reflective consciousness capable of making calculated choices on the basis of a pure activity of freedom.[23]

Emotional consciousness is just as much in bad faith as is the famous waiter who is only pretending to be a waiter, only role-playing his part. Emotional consciousness once entered into is sincere, it is truly believed in, but is not authentic. The emotional consciousness is by its very non-thetic unreflectiveness a conscious denial of itself and the freedom which it is. This is why Sartre can claim that emotional consciousness "is its own captive in the sense that it does not dominate its belief."[24] It denies its own freedom so that "freedom has to come from a purifying reflection or a total disappearance of the affecting situation."[25]

Emotional consciousness is an attempt to deny one's own condition, it is always an attempt to be what one is not. Anguish is the common emotional response to the realization of one's total ontological freedom and responsibility. By fleeing into anguish one attempts to refuse the responsibility which one has just realized one has, anguish is itself in bad faith as a denial of one's true condition.

Love is also in bad faith. In his description of love in Part III, Chapter Three of *Being and Nothingness*, Sartre states that in love consciousness attempts to possess the consciousness of the person loved without reducing this consciousness to an object. Consciousness wishes to merge with the other person into a unified whole. According to Sartre, "we have seen that this contingency (of otherness) is insurmountable; it is the *fact* of my relations with the other, just as my body is the *fact* of my being in the world. Unity with the other is therefore *in fact unrealizable in theory*, for the assimilation of the for-itself and the other in a single transcendence would necessarily involve the disappearance of the characteristic of otherness in the other."[26]

In other words, the choice to love is an unreflective attempt to become just what consciousness knows *in fact* that it is not, a unified whole with the other.

At this point, we could further delineate Sartre's description of love or of anguish from this perspective. On the other hand, we could go on to describe each of the other modes of emotional consciousness in accordance with this Sartrian model. However, we will not engage in any of these projects, worthwhile though they may be, because we have now answered the question posed at the beginning of this section. We now know that Sartre claims that emotional consciousness is a degradation of consciousness because it is in bad faith. We can further see that Sartre would respond to the criticism I present in section two of this article by pointing out that emotional consciousness is always ineffectual because it is always attempting to be something it knows it cannot be.

Sartre would not deny that many people very highly value emotional goals in their lives. However, Sartre would state that to the extent a person chooses to devote himself or herself to an emotional goal, that person can accurately be said to be in bad faith.

## IV

In this final section, what I wish to do is place Sartre's theory in the context of the traditional distinction between sense and sensibility. Furthermore, I wish to outline what I see as a possible way in which Sartre's theory could be further criticized.

What we have now seen is that Sartre regards pure reflection as ontologically superior not only to impure reflection, but also to the choice to spontaneously enter the emotional realm. Only in pure reflection do we authentically recognize consciousness as free and responsible, and only in pure reflection can we create our projects and go about attaining them in ways that are not in bad faith. Sartre does not claim that it is possible for anyone to totally avoid the bad faith of the emotional consciousness. He does suggest, however, that to the extent to which a person operates on the basis of pure reflection and avoids emotional responses, that person can accurately be described as being more or less authentic (i.e., in good faith) than other persons.

It is clear that Sartre's "pure reflection" plays the same role as "sense" in the traditional dichotomy between "sense and sensibility." Furthermore, while it is also clear that Sartre's "pure reflection" is significantly different from Aristotelian, Cartesian, or even Kantian rationality, it must be pointed out that in one fundamental aspect it is the same. Rationality for all of them, including Sartre, is the tool which allows us, to whatever degree such a thing is seen as possible, to reveal the true nature of our human condition in the world.

For Aristotle, rationality is the tool by which we come to empirically know ourselves and the world we live in. For Descartes, rationality is the tool by which we look within ourselves in order to come to know with certainty our own existence, the existence of God, and the nature of the world. For Kant, rationality is the tool which allows us to understand the limits of knowledge and the way in which ethics must function if it exists. Finally, in Sartre, rationality (i.e., pure reflection) is the tool which allows consciousness to reveal to itself its actual condition in all of its facticity, and in such a way as to free consciousness to create its own being authentically to the extent that such an activity is possible.

Sartre holds rationality to be ontologically superior to the emotions, much in the same way thinkers have traditionally done throughout the centuries. It is this fact which suggests the outline of a criticism of Sartre's position.

Sartre has claimed that he is presenting us with a phenomenological description of emotional consciousness. To the extent that he is presenting such a description, we would expect to be faced with a revelation of emotional consciousness as we actually experience it in our own lives. Such a description, by Sartre's own criteria, would not be tainted by the values which Sartre, as a private individual, has freely chosen to adopt for himself.

Yet, one cannot help but feel that Sartre has allowed some of his own personal values to seep into his description. Sartre has described the world (the in-itself) as inherently meaningless and absurd. Meaning is introduced into the world via consciousness (the for-itself) which is the origin of negation and, therefore, the creator of all value. To the extent that one denies one's total freedom to create one's values, and the full responsibility which goes hand in hand with that freedom, one can accurately be described as operating in bad faith. Sartre has gone on, as we have now seen, to describe the emotional consciousness as being in bad faith because it denies the possibility for consciousness to enter into pure reflection.

Yet, on the other hand, Sartre admits that consciousness freely chooses to enter the emotional realm. To the extent that consciousness freely makes such a choice, and also takes full responsibility for that choice, one can question whether consciousness is actually in bad faith. If I do not deny my possibility to enter pure reflection but simply choose not to do so in order to enter emotional consciousness, then why am I necessarily in bad faith? Am I not free to choose my project in any way that I wish?

A Sartrian might here respond that such a choice is spontaneous and non-thetic and, therefore, is a denial of consciousness' total freedom. I would respond that Sartre himself admits that one freely chooses to enter the emotional realm. The fact that such a choice is spontaneous and non-thetic does not constitute it as a denial of freedom. Consciousness can only be accused of denying its freedom if it enters the emotional realm in an unconscious fashion, (i.e., without making a choice). Sartre, however, vehemently denies that we undergo the emotions unconsciously. If we do choose to enter the emotional realm, then in what way is such a choice denial of our condition as free and responsible? Such a choice would appear only to be a denial of the thetic.

This leads one to question whether Sartre has any phenomenological basis for claiming an ontological superiority for the thetic over the non-thetic. Simply the fact that consciousness has the possibility of thetic reflection does not establish that it is in bad faith if it freely chooses to operate spontaneously.

Furthermore, Sartre has described love, as well as all other emotions, as an attempt to achieve a condition which is necessarily unachievable. I would here like to suggest, without pursuing this issue in detail, that Sartre's description of the experience of love is fundamentally flawed. While it is true that the experience of love is often a painful one, on the other hand, it cannot be denied that many people have had experiences of love which they have found extremely rewarding. To the extent that this is true, Sartre is placed in the uncomfortable position of denying the validity of experiences which others claim to have genuinely felt.

I have always taken the phenomenological method as a way of

describing consciousness as it is experienced. In that being in love is very often described as the most satisfying experience a person is capable of having, I would question a phenomenological description which designates that experience as inauthentic simply on the basis of what appears to be an extremely personalized account of the goals of love.

In other words, it seems to me Sartre has failed to be persuasively convincing in his portrayal of the emotions as always seeking to achieve the unachievable. This leads us to question Sartre's claim that pure reflection is in any way ontologically superior to emotional consciousness. In fact, if the world is indeed fundamentally meaningless, as Sartre claims, then one must wonder how any way of creating value which recognizes one's own freedom could be ontologically superior to any other way. As long as Sartre is willing to admit that consciousness freely chooses to enter the emotional realm, then I can see no ontological grounds for condemning such a choice.[28]

In conclusion, I would like to make very clear that I am not in any way rejecting Sartre's notion of "bad faith"; what I am questioning is Sartre's claim that the choice to enter the emotions is a choice *necessarily* made in bad faith. I further recognize that my outline of a criticism presented in this section is just that, an outline. More work is required to transform this outline into a full-blown critique of Sartre's theory, a critique which offers a plausible alternative to Sartre's theory. I hope to develop such a critique in the future.

NOTES

1 Here I refer to the inclusion of such notions as "eidetic structures" or "Being-in-the-world" with their obvious Husserlian and Heideggerian overtones.
2 Jean-Paul Sartre, *Being and Nothingness*, Washington Square Press, New York, 1971 (hereafter abbreviated as B. & N.), p. 806.
3 Jean-Paul Sartre, *The Emotions: Outline of a Theory*, Philosophical Library, New York, 1948 (hereafter abbreviated as E.), p. 63.
4 E., p. 61.
5 E., p. 70.
6 E., p. 75.
7 The role of the body is a complex and controversial one in Sartre's work. As this issue is not directly related to my discussion, I will not further explore it here.
8 E., p. 77.
9 E., p. 77.
10 E., p. 79.
11 E., p. 91.
12 E., p. 61.

13 E., p. 70.

14 The late Ernest G. Schachtel presented an excellent discussion of this point in his "Hope, Joy, and Pleasure," *Review of Existential Psychology and Psychiatry*, Vol. *XV*, Nos. 2, 3, 1977, p. 245-277.

15 B. & N., p. 218.

16 B. & N., p. 224.

17 B. & N., p. 236.

18 B. & N., p. 236.

19 B. & N., p. 225-26.

20 A full discussion of Sartrian "nihilation and temporality" will not be given here but can be found in B. & N., Part II, Chapters 2 and 3.

21 I shall not here engage in a full discussion of the relationship between pure phenomenology and regressive phenomenological psychology as such a discussion would be too lengthy and take us too far afield.

22 B. & N., p. 224.

23 Early in his work on the emotions (E., pp. 53-56), Sartre suggests that we can actively carry out the results of our reflection in a completely unreflective way. Such an unreflective following of the commands of reflection is not emotional, and thus, is not in bad faith. This unreflective activity escapes falling into bad faith because it is grounded in pure reflection whereas unreflective emotional activity is not.

24 E., p. 78.

25 E., p. 79.

26 B. & N., p. 477.

27 B. & N., p. 116f.

28 Marjorie Grene suggests a similar criticism of Sartre's theory in her article, "Sartre's Theory of the Emotions," Yale French Studies, Study #1, 1948, pp. 97-101.

## REFERENCES

Works by Jean-Paul Sartre

*Esquisse d'une théories des emotions*, Hermann, Paris, 1960; English Translation: *The Emotions: Outline of a Theory*, Philosophical Library, New York, 1948.

*L'Être et le Néant: Essai d'ontologie phénoménologique*, Librairie Gallimard, Paris, 1943; English Translation: *Being and Nothingness*, Washington Square Press, New York, 1971.

*L'Existentialisme est un Humanisme*, Librairie Gallimard, Paris, 1946; English Translation: *Existentialism and Humanism*, Haskell House Publishers Ltd., 1948.

*L'Imagination*, Librairie Gallimard, Paris, 1936; English Translation: *Imagination: A Psychological Critique*, University of Michigan Press, Ann Arbor, 1962.

# Good and Bad Faith: Weak and Strong Notions

JOSEPH S. CATALANO

I will distinguish in this paper two notions, or senses, of good and bad faith, "weak and strong," and I will attempt to establish that both senses function in Sartre's *Being and Nothingness* and are implied in much of his other writings.[1] I will begin with identifying the weak notions with what I call the "usual understanding" of these terms. Towards the end of the paper, however, it will become clear that, if one accepts the characterizations of the strong notions, that the original weak notions become altered and are no longer exactly equivalent to the "usual understanding" of these terms. I believe that the usual understanding of good and bad faith appear contradictory because they confuse notes of the weak and strong notions, notes that this paper attempts to separate. Thus the procedure will be to begin with a description of what I term the usual understanding of good and bad faith and to gradually show how these weak notions, even in their confused sense, imply strong notions. Once the strong notions have been delineated, they will then be compared with what I hope will be a more precise understanding of the weak notions. My purpose in elaborating these distinctions is to show that a viable strong notion of good faith exists only when contrasted with a strong notion of bad faith.

I call the usual acceptance of Sartre's notion of bad faith "weak" because it has a wide extension. Bad faith is seen in this view as a necessary aspect of the human condition, specifically, as the unsuccessful way in which we all must cope with our freedom by assuming roles in society. Given this weak sense of bad faith, good faith seems to be, at best, a momentary awakening, a fleeting glimpse of the futile character of our condition, a glimpse that never fully and never for very long escapes the conditions of bad faith itself. Nevertheless, even these weak senses of good and bad faith are not vacuous; they describe, in Sartre's philosophy, definite features of the human condition, features which I will now sketch and which I will later contrast with those characteristic of strong notions of good and bad faith.

I

It seems clear that, for Sartre, we can never escape role playing. He implies that, although we are free and responsible for the roles we play, our only option is to leave one role and enter another. True, once we realize that we have been playing a role and that we have passively accepted the way society sees and defines us, we may, in apparent good faith, react to this attempt of society to dominate our existence, and we may try to free ourselves from our acceptance of this domination, an acceptance that we now see as bad faith. But we will end in a new and different bad faith. Thus, in *Nausea*, the hero, Roquentin, gradually awakens from the slumbering acceptance of existence and from his own superficial attempts to give meaning to his life through travel and through the routine of writing a scholarly study of the Marquis de Rollebon. As an aspect of his awakening, the lives of his fellow citizens appear to him to be mannered, their voices hollow and their actions mechanical. He begins to see the bad-faith aspect of both their lives and his own, and he attempts to flee this vision. Towards the end of the book, Roquentin has a momentary intuition of the incredible gap between something and nothing; he faces the unconditional absurdity that anything should be. He further sees that this "brute" existence has been transformed into a world through human consciousness. His nausea is the realization that the world as a meaningful entity depends on the fact of human existence and freedom, facts which are themselves mere happenings. After this insight, Roquentin no longer seems to fit into society; he decides to write a novel in order to cope with his anguish, and, as Robert Denoon Cumming has noted, the book *Nausea* is itself the book that Roquentin decides to write at the end of the book.[2] But has Roquentin escaped bad faith? It would seem not. He has simply become a novelist and assumed a new role within the bad-faith society that he is condemning by his act of writing. Still, something did happen to him and his new life is not exactly the same as his former. Roquentin did not merely denounce himself for his bad faith; he changed his way of life. Nevertheless, insofar as his new life was also another role, Roquentin's good faith, in the final analysis, seems to have had very little significance for him.

This interpretation of the weak notions of good and bad faith can be supported by an analysis of the technical notion of bad faith introduced by Sartre in Part One of *Being and Nothingness*. In the context of Part One, the chapter on bad faith attempts to show that both negative statements as well as the absence and lack we find within the world originate from the nature of human consciousness as a "negative activity." One of the aspects of this negative activity is our ability to question freely the meaning of our existence including the issue itself of whether we are free. When we do so question, the ambiguity which results from this questioning can lead to anxiety and nausea. Further, according to Sartre, we can and frequently do flee from this anxiety, and this flight takes one of the several forms of lying to ourselves, or deceiving ourselves, about our freedom.

# GOOD AND BAD FAITH

There have been many attempts to explain how self-deception is possible and even a few attempts to show that it is impossible, but it would seem clear that, at the very least, we sometimes misunderstand the meaning of our behavior. For Sartre, self-deception and bad faith are the same, and, in what I call the weak sense of these terms, we can say that we cannot escape self-deception, or bad faith, because we go from one self-deception to another. Indeed in this context, Sartre sees sincerity itself to be a sign of bad faith. For example, we may sincerely admit to ourselves and to others that we are lazy. Our sincerity appears as honesty but it is an honesty that points away from our laziness and calls attention to our virtue of honesty. This apparent honesty is a subtle way of letting our laziness remain intact. It is a way of praising ourselves for our apparent self-knowledge. We see our sincerity as an ideal position from which we objectively judge our vices. What we do not admit is that our sincerity is also open to question because it is only a partial view of ourselves.³ Further, if we were truly honest about our condition we would attempt to change it rather than condemn ourselves for vices that we are retaining. In relation to the meaning of our behavior, it is our actions and not our abstract judgments about ourselves that are the best criteria for honesty. But, if it is true that our attempts to judge ourselves sincerely are in bad faith, it would seem that all self-knowledge is tainted with self-deception. Consequently, even our lucid understanding of ourselves points merely to the non-objectivity of our self-knowledge and to our awareness that there is no neutral position from which to examine our behavior. Again, in the weak sense, our good faith is only a fleeting realization that we cannot escape bad faith itself.

Our universal bad-faith condition can also be understood as calling attention to the way we continually "use up" our freedom by our actions and decisions. For Sartre, we can, loosely speaking, be said to have an essence insofar as we have a past, and the longer we live the more of a past we have. We are always free to redirect our lives and discover new meanings in our past, and no matter how great the "weight" of our past, we can always perform actions that are "out of character" and that are conversions to a new character. Nevertheless, we cannot escape the decisions we have made in the past; we cannot escape either the way or the extent to which we have used up our freedom. Also, we cannot avoid the way others see and objectify us. For example, for Sartre, the anti-Semite "overdetermines" the Jew. The Jew, however, cannot escape the overdetermination; he is free only to react to it authentically or inauthentically.⁴ Finally, this weak, universal sense of bad faith seems to be implied by Sartre's claim that man is a useless passion, and that we must act in anguish, abandonment and despair. Again accepting this universal, weak sense of bad faith, our good faith seems to be merely the Sisyphus-like struggle in which we are momentarily aware of the absurdity of our condition.

II

Although I believe there is validity to the usual interpretation of Sartre's notion of bad faith, I think that it misses the essential direction of his thought. Throughout much of Sartre's writings I believe that these weak notions point to and imply strong, limiting notions of both good and bad faith which I think it would be useful to introduce by an analogy.

There is, I think, a legitimate but "weak" sense in which we can say that we are all crazy, or insane. If we momentarily picture the meaning of our individual actions in relation to the world's activity they must at times appear to us to be futile if not ridiculous and crazy. Particularly those of us who are engaged in the academic professions must sometimes wonder about the meaning of our lives in the face of so much of the world's poverty, so much of the constant preparation for war and so much waste of human energy and resources. In the face of such insanity who can claim to be sane? Still, there are people who have a different and more specific type of insanity; there are people who suffer from so-called diseases such as schizophrenia and melancholia. They suffer from their insanity in a way in which we do not suffer from ours. We can of course say that there is no sense in trying to help them since we will be merely delivering them into another type of insanity. But this reasoning is sophistical. They have a right to live a more human existence even if this existence is itself from a different perspective a very crazy kind of existence. There is thus a strong, limiting notion of insanity and opposed to this notion there is a viable concept of sanity. Analogously, I believe that many of Sartre's writings refer to a strong, limiting notion of bad faith in relation to which there is implied a viable notion of good faith.

Before turning our attention to *Being and Nothingness*, I would like to illustrate how I see the strong notions of good and bad faith functioning in Sartre's *Anti-Semite and the Jew*. In portraying the anti-Semite, Sartre shows him to be a man who is afraid both of himself and of truth. He is afraid of himself because he is free, and he is afraid of truth because truth can be known only indefinitely. To hide from his fear, he fixes upon the Jew as a clear symbol of an evil that must be overcome in order to allow good to occur within the world. Once evil, symbolized by the Jew, is removed, the anti-Semite believes that the positive principle of good works automatically within the world. Sartre says:

82

> How can one choose to reason falsely? It is because of a longing for impenetrability. The rational man groans as he gropes for the truth.... But there are people who are attracted by the durability of a stone.... What frightens them is not the content of truth, of which they have no conception, but the form itself of truth, that thing of indefinite approximation. (pp. 18-19)

> A man who finds it entirely natural to denounce other men cannot have our conception of humanity; he does not see even those whom he aids in the same light as we do. His generosity, his kindness are not like our kindness, our generosity. You cannot confine passion to one sphere. (pp. 21-22)

> Anti-Semitism is thus seen to be at bottom a form of Manichaeism. It explains the course of the world by the struggle of the principle of Good with the principle of Evil.... Therefore Good consists above all in the destruction of Evil. Underneath the bitterness of the anti-Semite is concealed the optimistic belief that harmony will be re-established of itself, once Evil is eliminated. (pp. 40-43)

I believe that these quotes make it clear that Sartre is describing a specific type of consciousness. In the context of this paper, the anti-Semite is in bad faith in a very specific and strong sense of the term, otherwise, there would be no reason for Sartre to single him out for condemnation. Implicit, however, in this very condemnation of the anti-Semite is the realization that others can avoid a Manichaean outlook and practice good faith, also in a strong sense of that term.

Returning now to *Being and Nothingness*, I think that strong notions of good and bad faith are also implicit throughout Sartre's descriptive ontology. In this respect, I think that the chapter "Bad Faith" should be read as providing the foundation for describing two different ways in which consciousness can appear as a belief structure. By referring to consciousness as a belief structure, I am suggesting that Sartre sees belief as an intrinsic aspect of awareness. But I do not think it either necessary or fruitful to elaborate this claim here.[5] Nevertheless, at least the following should be noted: Belief is not distinguished from knowledge merely by a relation to an object; that is, for Sartre the intentional structure of consciousness requires that the *act* of believing be distinguished from the *act* of knowing. The point that I wish to make now is that I think this belief structure is itself further distinguished by Sartre into two basic types. The intentional structure of a bad-faith belief is fundamentally different from the intentional structure of a good-faith belief; that is, persons in bad faith are distinguished not only by *what* they believe but by the *way* they believe.

I think that Sartre lays the foundation for the description of good and bad faith as two fundamentally different ways of believing in the chapter, "Bad Faith," in *Being and Nothingness*.

> Bad faith does not hold the norms and criteria of truth as they are accepted by the critical thought of good faith. What it decides first, in fact, is the nature of truth. With bad faith a truth appears, a method of thinking, a type of being which is like that of objects.... Consequently a peculiar type of evidence appears; non-persuasive evidence.... Thus bad faith in its primitive project and in its coming into the world decides on the exact nature of its requirements. It stands forth in the firm resolution *not to demand too much*, to count itself satisfied when it is barely persuaded, to force itself in decisions to adhere to uncertain truths. This original project of bad faith is a decision in bad faith on the nature of faith. (BN p. 68)

I take the last sentence of the above quote to be crucial. "This original project of bad faith is a decision in bad faith on the nature of faith." Good and bad faith are thus distinguished not by their relation to objects, but by their relation to faith itself. Abstracting from the problem of what is meant by describing good and bad faith as "decisions," and turning our attention merely to how they are distinguished as beliefs, we see that in a very simple sense good faith is a critical faith and bad faith an uncritical faith. The uncritical aspect of bad faith consists in the way it "views" the nature of faith or belief itself. One consequence of this is that bad faith does not recognize its own uncritical stance because its global view includes an "appropriate" view of criteria. Of course, all belief is based on probable evidence and there are no *a priori* criteria to measure the critical claims of this evidence. A bad-faith consciousness, in the strong sense of the term, must, I think, be pictured as one that alters the nature of evidence for its own purposes. This device can succeed and not collapse into a mere cynical awareness of cheating because the evidence for belief is indeed ambiguous: belief can never be totally justified.[6] Indeed, Sartre suggests that the person in bad faith, in the strong sense of this term, uses the ambiguity in the nature of belief for his own purposes. If there are no absolute ideals, then there are no absolute criteria and the person in bad faith is free to believe that anything goes in the realm of belief. The person in bad faith does not explicate this attitude; rather he turns his mind away from the glimpses of his condition. Ironically, this individual is usually the type of person who seems to need absolute ideals, and since these are lacking in the world he both creates them where he needs them and believes that they were really there for him to find.

Within the context of *Being and Nothingness*, the full sense of the strong notion of bad faith is, I think, not elaborated until the section, "Existential Psychoanalysis," in Part Four. Indeed, I think that it is crucial to read Sartre's chapter on bad faith in conjunction with all of Part Four. Here it becomes clear to what extent Sartre's view of consciousness must be understood in relation to Freud's view. In opposition to Freud, Sartre claims that we choose our neurosis. Here again, I think that it is useful to distinguish a weak and strong sense of "neurosis." Although we all have some psychic abberations, I understand Sartre in this section to be concerned mainly with a definite, limiting notion of a neurosis as a deep, self-deception. Thus speaking of an inferiority complex Sartre says: "This inferiority which I struggle against in which nevertheless I recognize, this I have chosen from the start" (BN p. 459). A simple example may illustrate how I think this "choice" might occur: Imagine that a child has studied and then failed his first examination in mathematics. This failure could be a crucial experience for the child; he may have to face the possibility that in the future even his best efforts in mathematics as well as in other areas may result in failure. Of course, this one failure gives little evidence for his chances of performing successfully in the future; but for the child this evidence may appear sufficient to justify rejecting future efforts with their possibilities of failure. In fact, there is some evidence to show that through no fault of his own either nature or circumstances caused him to perform poorly in mathematics. But if this is the case, then why study? If the child "reasons" in this way he will of course fail future examinations, thereby generating the needed evidence to believe that through no fault of his own he lacks ability in mathematics. In later life it may be useful or necessary for him to learn mathematics and he may now use his "will power" to conquer his "lack of ability" in mathematics. Here, Sartre agrees with Freud that the individual who thus struggles with himself is not attacking the right problems and even if he does succeed in conquering his "inability" to learn mathematics another psychic abberation will occur until he confronts the early experience he is avoiding. Of course, for Freud, the early experience this individual refuses to face is not directly related to mathematics; for Sartre, on the contrary, the early experience is precisely his "choice" to believe uncritically in his own lack of ability in mathematics. Indeed, for Sartre, this inferiority complex may be a device for hiding a desire to be superior. An extreme fear of failure could cover a desire to achieve and, in this interpretation, the inferiority complex is self-deceptive in its very project. The child implicitly desires to perform successfully but fearing failure creates the evidence that he would have been able to succeed if circumstances and nature had not been against him. He can thus retain the simultaneous belief in his superior abilities and his justification for not even attempting to perform in accordance with these abilities. Further, if at some later time he should "sincerely" claim to desire to conquer his inferiority complex, in this case his mental block in mathematics, without admitting his original flight from effort and fear of failure, his "sincerity" is in bad faith, in the strong sense of that term.

*Joseph Catalano*

### III

I would like to conclude this sketch by trying to make the strong notions of good and bad faith somewhat clearer. Towards the end, I will briefly compare the strong notions with the revised senses of the weak notions alluded to at the beginning of this paper.

It is clear that we cannot at every moment question the roles we play in society and the meaning of our existence. The possibility for questioning is always there, and this is sufficient for making us responsible for continuing in the roles we have chosen. We must choose to play roles but everything depends on how we are placed in reference to our roles. If we accept our roles as given to us by nature or society, whereas in fact we have chosen them, then we live in bad faith, in the strong sense of that term. In this case, we do not face what Sartre calls our "fundamental choice," rather we view our freedom to concern merely our deliberations about actions within our role. This freedom, however, is deceptive; it limits us to the relatively minor choices within our present role and thus hides our responsibility for choosing the role itself. Sartre says that when we deliberate "the chips are down," and he means that generally our deliberations keep our larger life-style fixed, as when a professor of philosophy deliberates about what textbook to use, and never questions his role in society as a professor. For Sartre, this "freedom" is uninteresting and, for the most part, predictable. But if our professor of philosophy were to decide to make his way in the world as a painter, this "choice," or conversion, would represent a real use of freedom. In this instance, the deliberations that preceded the conversion might later make the conversion reasonable but they could never fully account for it because, before the change, all deliberations were colored by the former life-style. In such a case there is a genuine leap. But the above description has to be qualified. Leaps are rare and it would thus seem that we would seldom be in a position to exercise our real freedom. This is not completely true. Sartre's point I think is that glimpses of the possibility of a radical change surface now and then from beneath our everyday choices. The professor of philosophy, who is deliberating about what textbook to use, will at times realize that this everyday choice is also a way of choosing to continue his life-style as a college professor, and this choice to continue his role is interesting and significant. To try to make our description clearer here, we can attempt to visualize our professor continuing his life-style in either a good or bad faith way. This portrait, however, will be based on a supposition: We must assume that anyone living a relatively comfortable life will have glimpses of a larger social context in which he can see his own life-style as a "role" and visualize real alternative possibilities for himself. Given this supposition, the professor, in good faith, will *at times* allow himself to hold and reflect upon these fleeting glimpses that his life-style is a role that can be changed. For it may happen that social conditions would cause the continuing in such a role to be unreasonable. The professor, in bad faith, should be visualized as one whose habitual way of life turns him from facing these glimpses of the larger context which would reveal his life-style as a role. Further, and this is the precise difference between good and bad faith, the professor living in bad faith can continue in his life-style because he has an altered notion of belief that itself hides from him his uncritical life-style. This uncritical stance, however, seems to go against the natural tendency of consciousness to question itself, and thus, according to Sartre, the individual living in bad faith will experience moments of anxiety.

In the strong sense of these terms, good and bad faith thus appear as two different ways of coping with the ambiguity that is inherent in every act of belief. Good faith accepts ambiguity and does not use it as an excuse for being uncritical; bad faith uses ambiguity for its own purposes of justifying its uncritical attitudes. One way of understanding how this uncritical stance can be sustained is to visualize a bad-faith attitude as projecting an impossible ideal of good faith. If the *ideal* of good faith is seen as impossible to attain, then bad faith is free to disregard the uncritical aspect of its own belief.[7] Indeed, bad faith can be thus understood as a belief that since real good faith is impossible bad faith is also impossible. That is, belief is simply belief and one belief is as good as another. To repeat, bad faith can sustain itself as a true belief because there are, in fact, no absolute or *a priori* criteria by which to classify beliefs as critical or uncritical. Still there is a world of difference between one who attempts to have reasonable beliefs and one who avoids the effort because there are no initial guarantees that reason will arrive at the truth. To belabor the point with one further example: A soldier may say that his role is to obey orders and that if everyone questioned superiors all the time there would be anarchy. But it is ever an issue of questioning all orders all the time or is this reasoning used as an excuse to relieve him of the burden of living with the possibility that he may have to question orders sometimes?

I think that the same strong notions of good and bad faith can be seen in Sartre's *Nausea*. It is clear to me that Roquentin does not, at the end of the novel, return to the same bad faith that he was living in the beginning of the novel. At first, he was hiding from his freedom, and living a life characterized by a strong sense of bad faith. At the end of the book, he does indeed return to a role, as we must all do, but I believe that there is a basic difference. Now he is no longer hiding from his freedom; rather he has consciously chosen a role, a role that like all others does not give a perfect solution to the danger of hiding from responsibility. There is no role that, of itself, gives meaning to life.[8]

But a life of good faith, in the strong sense, is one that attempts to better a world laden with roles determined by others. The first step to accomplish this is to realize that the roles of society are not fixed by nature, and this is what Roquentin realizes at the end of the novel. The mirror that his writings presents to himself and to the world is not a conclusion but a beginning from which change is possible. But the world is laden with an "archeology" of meanings, and Roquentin must be prepared for a continual awakening to the extent to which he still views aspects of life as "natural" when in fact they are merely roles determined by society. Nevertheless, it is his conversion to good faith that prepares him to recognize this latent "bad faith."[9] Further, I believe that it is this strong sense of good faith that has allowed Sartre to recognize that aspects of his early views were in bad faith. For example, Sartre apparently later realized that his descriptions of freedom in *Being and Nothingness* assumed a certain openness as natural to society when in fact it merely reflected his own relatively comfortable, cosmopolitan life. Thus he sees a progression from "bad faith" to good faith in the views on freedom expressed first in *Being and Nothingness* and later in such works as *St. Genet*, and in the *Critique of Dialectical Reason*. This progression, however, follows directly from the strong notion of good faith implied in *Being and Nothingness*.

I think that the weak and strong senses of good and bad faith are related. The weak sense of bad faith calls attention to the tendency and danger to flee from the ambiguity that results from the fact that so much of our existence is based on belief. Bad faith, in the weak sense, thus calls attention to the possibility of bad faith, in the strong sense. Clearly, however, one can live in bad faith, in the weak sense, while also living in good faith, in the strong sense.

But we may still question the suitableness of calling the general human condition "bad faith," even in a weak sense of this term. The question of suitableness is indeed an open question; the term, however, does point to a particular aspect of the life that we live in our present society. Society makes it very difficult for the average person to question the meaning of life and the values of role-playing. We are not here concerned with the obvious benefits that we derive from society. The issue is the ease in which present society can alter human consciousness and role-playing so that it seems natural to do what is clearly wrong. That the *Third Reich* happened confronts philosophy with a fact that cannot be ignored, namely, that, in the concrete, there is inherent in today's society a tendency to buy security at any price and to believe that this purchase is reasonable. The issue is not whether human nature is corrupt, but whether the average individual will make the effort needed to live a free life. When society makes it difficult for individuals to follow their own consciousness, it seems to be an historical fact that few will do so. If this tendency in human nature is called "bad faith," it is done, I believe, as a warning that society itself must be open and encourage questioning if the average person is to avoid living a life of bad faith, in the strong sense of the term.

I realize that in mentioning the social dimension I have already altered my original model, and it is clear to me that this dimension is needed for the full picture of good and bad faith. Indeed, within the context of Sartre's philosophy, a further, and I think useful, distinction would have to be made between good and bad faith and authenticity and inauthenticity to complete the picture. Thus the present descriptions must be taken as abstract. They describe, for the most part, partial aspects of two basic ways in which a person, in a generally open society, can manifest his beliefs and freedom. For even in an open society a free life is a task that some in good faith embrace and others in bad faith flee.

### NOTES

1 In an earlier paper, "On the Possibility of Good Faith" (*Man and World*, vol. 13, no. 2, 1980), I tried to show that a textual analysis of the chapters, "Bad Faith" and "Existential Psychoanalysis" in Sartre's *Being and Nothingness*, implies a viable notion of good faith. In this paper I will attempt to locate my textual analysis within a wider context of Sartre's writings.

2 *Cf. The Philosophy of Jean-Paul Sartre* edited and introduced by Robert Denoon Cumming. (New York: Random House, 1965), p. 14.

3 Also, our so-called sincerity often hides the fact that we choose the vices that we admit to. Thus, in *The Flies* trans. Stuart Gilbert. (New York: Alfred Knopf), p. 92, Sartre writes:

> "Electra: Note her words, Philebus. That's a rule of the game. People will beg you to condemn them, but you must be sure to judge them only on the sins they own to; their other evil deeds are no one's business, and they wouldn't thank you for detecting them."

4 *See* Jean-Paul Sartre, *Anti-Semite and the Jew*, trans. George J. Becker (New York: Schocken Books, 1948), pp. 79-141. (All further references will be to this edition.) Sartre does not appear concerned to develop consistently the distinction between authenticity and inauthenticity on the one hand and good and bad faith on the other hand. Still I suspect that his views can be shown to be consistent. In *Being and Nothingness* he clearly states that authenticity and inauthenticity are moral categories and, as such, do not belong in a descriptive ontology as does the phenomenon of bad faith. In *Anti-Semite and the Jew*, however, Sartre seems to clearly portray the anti-Semite as in bad faith and as reprehensible. Further, the question of authenticity does not arise in reference to the anti-Semite but in relation to the Jew. The bad faith of the anti-Semite creates the situation in which the Jew must now respond either authentically or inauthentically. I think Sartre's point is that objectively the consciousness of the anti-Semite is a wrongly directed, global and pre-reflective orientation to the world; never-

## Joseph Catalano

theless, it will always be an open question to what extent the anti-Semite is responsible for his condition. Thus regardless of the guilt of the anti-Semite, his pre-reflective bad-faith condition creates the situation in which the Jew, on the reflective and thus the moral level, must respond either authentically or inauthentically.

5 What I am suggesting is that belief, for Sartre, is consciousness itself as viewed from a certain aspect. In particular, belief refers to the relation, within the pre-reflective cogito, of the non-thetic self to its ideal selfhood. That is, our "project" is a belief structure. Still I think that Sartre's view of good and bad faith has significance independent of this ontology. Cf Jean-Paul Sartre *Being and Nothingness* trans. Hazel Barnes (New York: Philosophical Library, 1956), pp. 47-105. See also my *Commentary on Jean-Paul Sartre's "Being and Nothingness,"* (New York: Harper & Row, 1974; Reprinted with a new introduction; Chicago: University of Chicago Press, 1980), pp. 78-110.

6 It is frequently stated that Sartre has given us an excellent description of self-deception, but has not shown us how it is possible. But I think that Sartre has shown us how at least some deep self-deception can occur. Indeed, as I hope will become apparent, I see bad faith, in the strong sense, as a specific type of deep-rooted self-deception. The point that is overlooked, even by Fingarette's generally sympathetic treatment, (Herbert Fingarette, *Self-Deception*. New York: 1969) is that Sartre's paradoxical way of describing consciousness is not due to his inordinate love of colorful language, but is rather meant to point to a paradoxical aspect of consciousness itself. Briefly, for Sartre, every belief in $p$ implies a nonbelief in $p$. That is, we can never so believe in $p$ that we entirely eliminate the attitude of not believing in $p$; further, it is only by an effort, that is characteristic of bad faith, that we maintain a seeming unwavering belief in $p$. Thus to *begin* an analysis of self-deception by describing it simply as a simultaneous belief in $p$ and *not-p*, is to impose a simplicity and homogeneity to consciousness that may make self-deception impossible to explain philosophically.

7 In my article, "On the Possibility of Good Faith," *op. cit.*, I presented a more detailed analysis of the distinction between the ideal of good faith and good faith. Further, I also tried to indicate how "will power" acts to accomplish the self-deception that is bad faith, in the strong sense of that term.

8 In the concrete, one always determines the meaning of a life with a role but the role does not, of itself, give meaning to a life.

9 That is, "bad faith" in the *new*, weak sense referred to in the beginning of this article.

# Boredom and the Yawn*

LINDA BELL

Yawns come in a variety of shapes and sizes. They appear at various times, and in many different places. Yawns open more than mouths; they open also the possibility of analysis. They can be elucidated aesthetically, clinically, ethically, sociologically, and probably even politically. A yawn may tell us one of a number of things: that the yawner is sleepy, that he or she is not getting enough oxygen, or that he or she is bored. While the yawn of boredom may initially not look very interesting, appearances here are deceptive. As paradoxical as it may seem, boredom is not itself boring. It is, in fact, a fascinating subject — especially to a phenomenologist.

Fortunately, the contemporary phenomenologist who undertakes to examine the yawn need not begin with an unexplored chasm. The investigative gap has been partially filled by Jean-Paul Sartre's analyses in his novel *Nausea*, though much more work remains to be done.

Sartre is noted for his brilliant and profound descriptions of a wide variety of human phenomena. In *Being and Nothingness*, for example, he has carefully and perceptively depicted the shame of the individual who, while looking through the keyhole, realizes that he in turn is being observed by another, the self-deception of the waiter in the cafe, as well as that of the woman with her would-be lover. Similarly sensitive and revealing is his analysis of the yawn of boredom.

Antoine Roquentin, the diarist of *Nausea*, is in Bouville, a town where little if anything ever seems to happen, studying M. de Rollebon, a somewhat shadowy figure of minor historical significance. He is bored with Bouville, with M. de Rollebon.[1] He is even bored with his life of "eat, sleep, sleep, eat."[2] He declares: "I am bored, that's all. From time to time I yawn so widely that tears roll down my cheek. It is a profound boredom, profound, the profound heart of existence, the very matter I am made of."[3]

This is not simple, everyday boredom; it is, Sartre tells us "profound boredom." And it is profound not only in its intensity, as indicated by tears running down Roquentin's cheeks, but also in revealing a deep and seldom noticed aspect of things.[4] It is precisely this awareness, profoundly felt, which constitutes nausea, an experience which provides a unique

*For their encouragement and helpful comments, I am indebted to Professors John Beversluis, Calvin O. Schrag, William L. McBride, and Joseph S. Catalano. The initial draft of this paper was written during a National Endowment for the Humanities Summer Seminar, "Philosophical Anthropology in Recent Continental Thought," directed by Professor Schrag. An earlier version of this paper was read at the Southern Society for Philosophy and Psychology, April 12, 1969, Norfolk, Virginia.

access to an existence which usually hides itself: as the "veneer" of diversity—the individuality of the root, the park gates, the bench, the grass—vanishes, existence unveils itself as "the very paste of things...soft, monstrous masses, all in disorder—naked, in a frightful, obscene nakedness."⁵

This experience of nausea is closely connected, in Sartre's thought, with the yawn. Like Camus' feeling of unfamiliarity, it signifies a breaking-down of the normal way of seeing things in their familiar individuality.⁶ Unlike Camus' feeling of unfamiliarity, however, Sartre's nausea is not merely an awareness of the inhuman aspect of things, other persons, and one's self: an experience of "nature without humanity."⁷ It is also an actual experience of, a privileged access to, the very being of things, the in-itself of *Being and Nothingness*. In nausea, one feels the unbearable "touch" of objects, one's unbearable connection with them.⁸

Admittedly nausea is a unique boredom—as Sartre says, a "profound boredom." It provides access to the very being of things and thereby may lead us to an awareness of ourselves as the source of meaning and value in the world. Nausea is primarily an experience of the in-itself. Is this true of all boredom?

I realize that such a question may seem strange to anyone familiar with Sartre's accounts of our bad faith flights from freedom and responsibility and of our reactions in shame, arrogance, love, language, masochism, indifference, desire, hate, and sadism to the looks of others. Given these analyses, it may seem obvious that boredom, and hence the bored yawn, must always be connected ultimately with the in-itself—the being of things—and not with the for-itself—the nothingness of consciousness. Or, to formulate the issue with respect to ourselves and others, it may appear self-evident that boredom must be connected with facticity—that aspect of ourselves most closely connected with the being of things—and not with freedom and transcendence.

Given these analyses, it seems that one can be bored with oneself and with others only in certain restricted ways, that is, only with the facticity, past, and object-side of each. Accordingly, one could become bored with one's own or another's situation, with either's body, class, and economic status, or with what either has managed to make of himself, with past and present accomplishments, or with the way each sees or is seen by the other. What appears impossible is that one could be bored with the freedom and transcendence of oneself or of another. It is just this that I want to challenge.

With respect to one's own freedom, Sartre proposes that one may respond with despair, anguish, and a sense of abandonment.⁹ Unwilling to recognize and accept the extent of one's freedom and responsibility, an individual may flee in bad faith from the recognition of his freedom, hiding behind excuses which he himself in some sense knows to be illegitimate. He may become, for example, a "serious man," a man who regards his values as given and ready-made and his imperatives as unquestioned and even unquestionable. Surely Sartre is right that boredom is possible here. The serious individual is almost certainly bound to be boring to others, if not to himself.

One may, however, flee one's freedom in a radically different way. Sartre's examples of the woman with her would-be lover and of the homosexual are examples of individuals who try to escape their freedom and its consequent responsibility by emphasizing freedom itself, but in a very restricted sense. They try to treat themselves as abstract freedom and thus to deny the concrete freedoms that they are. Wanting to postpone the moment of decision, the woman refuses to recognize the implicit commitment she makes as she leaves her hand "between the warm hands of her companion."[10] She divorces herself from her body by drawing her companion into a lofty and sentimental discussion of "Life" and of her life in particular. Thus, her hand does not commit her; as a mere thing, it can neither consent to nor resist the man's advances.

Similarly, Sartre's homosexual refuses, in spite of the urging by his critic (the "champion of sincerity"), to admit that he is a homosexual. Refusing to acknowledge a past of homosexual activities, he affirms his freedom. In ignoring his past, this affirmation is at best an affirmation of an abstract freedom.

These individuals who paradoxically flee their freedom and responsibility by fleeing into their freedom and transcendence, away from their facticity, thereby resemble Kierkegaard's aesthete. And it is significant that it is the aesthete who, in Kierkegaard's presentation, is plagued by boredom. The aesthete does everything in his power to avoid commitment: he guards against friendship, avoids marriage, never accepts appointment to official positions, and engages in all sorts of unproductive activities to keep himself active in a way that is compatible with his leisure. Yet he is bored: he cares for nothing; his view of life is "utterly meaningless;"[11] "life has become a bitter drink."[12] He says, "How terrible tedium is—terribly tedious. ...[T]he only thing I see is emptiness, the only thing I move about in is emptiness."[13] The aesthete finds himself and others boring: "all men are bores."[14] Boredom entered the world with Adam and only increased proportionately as the population increased.[15]

I find it significant that Kierkegaard recognizes boredom as a problem for the aesthete but not for Judge William, the "moral man" of Volume II of *Either/Or*. The moral man, like Sartre's serious man, flees from his freedom to his facticity and hides behind what he is, his status in the community, what he has been, what is expected of him, his marriage, and the comfortable conformity with the status quo which is encouraged by the moral imperative's demand of universalizability. At best only slightly troubled by the country pastor's affirmation that "against God we are always in the wrong,"[16] Judge William is certainly not troubled by boredom in spite of the fact that his self-righteousness and myopically moral advice make him, for many of us, "an intolerable bore."[17]

This seems to be exactly the opposite of what we would expect. The individual who flees into abstract freedom and becomes "fantastic" is the one who may become the more bored. He spends his time entertaining himself, existing in the abstract, languishing in his weightlessness. Of course, his is really not a genuine sense and utilization of freedom inasmuch as he uses his freedom as a way to avoid confronting himself and acknowledging the necessity of choosing. Still, though, the mere fact that Kierkegaard recognizes such a threat of boredom in this level of existence suggests that the connection of boredom with facticity far from exhausts the phenomenon of boredom.

Of greater importance is the question of what happens if an individual does not flee his freedom and transcendence but rather confronts them authentically. Many see problems at this point, fearing that one must choose between the serious and what Kierkegaard calls the "hypothetical self": a self which "...does not for an instant stand firm...[since it] exercises quite as much the power of loosing as of binding, every instant it can quite arbitrarily begin all over again...."[18] A hypothetical person is, like Dostoevsky's Underground Man, always so painfully and explicitly aware that he and he alone must choose and thereby create his own foundations for acting that he can never act. Since, before acting, he must always first question his earlier decision to act, he cannot escape from this never-ending need to reaffirm his previous choice. He knows all too well that he can tear down as arbitrarily as he has built, that he remains free to reject what he has previously accepted and to accept what he has rejected.

It seems possible, however, for Sartre to escape this alleged dilemma of the ready-made values of the serious, on the one hand, and the paralysis of the constant reevaluation of the hypothetical, on the other. Sartre's reasons for rejecting the serious have already been examined. In addition, Sartre could deal with the hypothetical man's infinite postponement of action in much the same way that a utilitarian such as Bentham deals with the alleged need to calculate the pleasurable and painful consequences of every possible action in a given situation. Like Bentham, Sartre could point out that we are responsible for our postponement of decision and our inaction, which is just to say that we choose to postpone, to requestion, and to calculate, rather than to act in some other way.

Although Sartre would thus reject both horns of this dilemma, a question nevertheless remains as to what the third (and authentic) alternative would be. Clearly, the authentic individual must recognize and affirm his or her freedom. Initially, this accepting recognition would no doubt be as exhilarating as the rejecting recognition of freedom was terrifying for the individual in bad faith. In recognizing one's freedom in this authentic way, an individual may be enormously elated. He or she may spin dizzily with the awareness that one is not just one's facticity: one's class, what one has been, one's body, etc. One may be brought out of this vertigo to some degree by a sense of responsibility as one recognizes the extent of one's freedom and that one is without excuse. He or she must not, however, allow this sense of responsibility to pull him or her back into the serious. In particular, he or she must resist the temptation to take his own past decisions as irrevocably binding him or her in the present.

To avoid the extremes of the serious and the hypothetical, a certain combination of playfulness and boredom seems necessary. An individual needs to be able to regard past choices with a detachment that always enables one to question and to reexamine them, and one even needs to encourage oneself constantly to do so. At the same time, one must be able to carry through on at least some of one's projects, even though he or she may realize that he or she has the freedom (and often may choose) not to do so.

Repetition has its proper place in the sphere of the ethical, and Kierkegaard's Judge William recognizes this. If the serious is to be avoided, though, this repetition must be undertaken with an attitude less serious than that of Judge William: it must involve something like the spirit of play, though not frivolity. In a game, one always—at least as long as one is playing and not seriously involved (in what is no longer a game)—retains an awareness that one could stop the game or at any rate get out at any point.[19] The sense of free involvement is paramount in play; and to the extent that it is lacking, we are doing something other than playing, for example, trying to win, to impress, to gain a scholarship, to convince ourselves of our ability. This does not mean that one cannot play a spirited and vigorous game. Nor does it mean that one cannot get bored and yet carry on the game. In fact, many a game is finished in boredom for no better reason than that it was begun. Many a project is completed in boredom for no better reason than that it was undertaken.

We may indeed find good and compelling reasons to end a game or to discontinue a project. But must we *always* have good reasons for carrying through what we previously judged to be right or even obligatory? For every "Why?" there is a "Why not?" which may be just as difficult to answer. Unlike the endlessly questioning "Why?" of the Underground Man, play and boredom do not paralyze but may allow us not only to initiate action but also to follow it through to completion.

To play, then, is to freely engage in an activity. Play is neither serious nor agonizingly hypothetical. It involves both the recognition that one is free and an affirmation of one's subjectivity. Some sort of distance from the activity is necessary for play. Those who are too intimately identified with their tasks do not play. Neither do they become bored since it is also distance which allows the individual to become bored. Given the requisite distance, it seems impossible to rule out the possibility of boredom wherever there is play. Why, then, may not an authentic individual occasionally become bored with the use of freedom just as the aesthete becomes bored with abstract freedom?

Why should not the initial exhilaration of the awareness of freedom settle down into the humdrum? Everything else does; why should this be an exception? Camus concludes that we must imagine Sisyphus as happy as he descends to retrieve his stone. Surely it is just as necessary to imagine Sisyphus as at least occasionally bored. Cannot Sisyphus yawn from boredom as he descends to retrieve his stone at the foot of the hill, even though he knows that he and he alone chooses thus to resist the meaninglessness of the universe, attempting in his rebellion to impose a human stamp on what is and will remain alien and inhuman? Cannot an individual occasionally be bored as he pours water through sieves, although he may choose this and may deem it in the circumstances the most important thing to do? Surely in such cases of boredom one is bored with one's freedom and not just with the contingency of the particular choice (that it need not have been) nor with the necessity of making some choice or other (in the sense of being condemned to freedom).

There is some indication that Sartre recognized this possibility in authenticity. In *Being and Nothingness*, he is very clear about the connection between play and authenticity, noting that a special study of play belongs to an ethics.[20] Moreover, in *Saint Genet*, Sartre presents a dialectic of authenticity at the end of which, as he so dramatically asserts, Genet "becomes a man."[21] What happens to Genet at this point, though, is revealing. He settles down into a rather humdrum existence; Genet the homosexual and thief marries and takes on the responsibilities of a family. In one sense, little remains to be said about him; he is no longer so interesting. But in another sense, much remains to be said, for he has become a man, an authentic human being.

There is also the possibility—as yet unexamined—of the bored yawn as a response to the other. Again, Sartre's analyses suggest that such boredom is a response to the facticity, past, and object-side of the other. Thus, Roquentin is bored with M. de Rollebon who, being dead, is pure facticity, past, and object-side. Roquentin experiences nausea, for example, as he becomes aware of another as having "barely a face," with "his hand like a fat white worm in my own hand,"[22] or as he imagines the flesh of a woman's husband as "defenceless, bloated, slobbering, vaguely obscene."[23] Once again, though, the completeness of Sartre's analyses needs to be questioned. Is this all there is to the yawn as a response to another? Again, I think not.

Surely we cannot deny that we often respond to others as Sartre has suggested. One may indeed experience the inhuman and alien in another. One may feel the superfluity of the other. One may become bored with another's facticity, past, and object-side. For the most part, individuals may react in bad faith to the look of another. They may not want to assume their responsibility for the object-sides the other in some sense gives them. As they flee from this recognition, they may very well not be bored. They may be much too serious about their undertakings.

But what if someone does not flee in such seriousness? What if he accepts his freedom and his responsibility even for the way others see him? Does he not then react rather differently to the look of the other? As Sartre recognizes in *Being and Nothingness*, to react in indifference, in effect pretending that one is not looked at, is a reaction of flight, of bad faith. Surely, however, boredom is a very different and often appropriate response. Sartre considers instances of the look in which an individual has been seen in a way he does not wish to be seen. Even without turning to a consideration of authentic response to the other, we might suggest cases in which the look of the other is not particularly threatening. For example, even this kind of bad faith is unmoved when the look of the other is particularly distorting. For example, a look will not be particularly threatening, bad faith notwithstanding, if the one who looks is notoriously insensitive and imperceptive and if it is quite clear that what he or she thinks is seen bears no resemblance whatsoever to what is actually going on.

If an individual is authentic and not fleeing freedom and responsibility, the situation is somewhat similar. One's interest in the other's look would be in direct proportion to the latter's sensitivity and perceptiveness. One must, after all, minimally recognize oneself in what the other sees; and in the effort fully to assume responsibility for his or her object-side, the authentic individual has little if anything to learn about himself or herself from someone who so distorts those seen that they are simply unable to recognize these views of them as in any way their object-sides.

Here a response of boredom seems not only expected but even most appropriate. This fact might explain why, even in bad faith, we are so uninterested in and unthreatened by some, even by some who try so hard to interest or to threaten us. Sartre himself allows that what is threatening about the look is that the other therein discloses to the one seen the latter's object-side. If one's object-side is not disclosed by what one originally might have taken as a look, then it no doubt was not a real look. Although it may disclose one's object-side in the same way as a rustling leaf, taken as an other-looking-at-one, nevertheless the actual look of the other may turn out to be itself no more threatening or enticing than the leaf.

Perhaps we can carry Sartre's analysis a step further. Not only may we not be interested in the way the other sees us, but also we may even not be at all interested in the other's freedom and transcendence. It may be true that he or she organizes the world around himself or herself just as we each organize it around ourselves. It may very well be that the other in some sense usurps our possibilities by subsuming them under his or her projects. But the question is, must we be threatened or even moderately interested in this? May we not be bored with the freedom and transcendence of the other?

Is it just that we feel that we know in advance what the other is going to do? That may be a part of it, in which case boredom results from others' predictability. This looks once again like we are bored with something resembling or closely connected with others' facticity, their past, and the way we see them, rather than with their freedom and transcendence. But others may truly do the unexpected, and we may still be bored with them. They may be reeling about with the anxiety of facing their own freedom; a world as it were of possibilities may be confronting them; and we may nevertheless be bored with them. Whereas we may be fascinated with the cyclical patterns in nature, the repetitions in animal life, and even the spinning of a top, we may be bored to tears by a human freedom, unpredictable though it may be.

A final point needs to be made in connection with boredom as a response to another, especially in its physical manifestation of the yawn. Sartre has a great deal to say in general about holes. Man himself, according to Sartre, is a hole in being, and this accounts for the all too human fascination with holes and for man's constant striving to fill them. In a philosophy so concerned with the significance of holes, it is remarkable that we do not find any mention of the yawn — particularly the yawn as a response to another — as a hole. This is even more remarkable when one attends to the actual role a yawn may play in the encounter between the self and another.

Here indeed is an interesting hole, one that, as we have seen, can in a sense swallow the look of the other. Someone looks at another. The latter yawns. The look of the first is lost: where he or she had tried to objectify the other, there is no other to be objectified. The other has removed himself or herself; he or she is no longer there at all. What remains are tongue, lips, and tonsils. The yawner has removed himself or herself from the antagonism directed toward him or her, from the circle into which the look might have precipitated the two of them. Thus, the yawn enables one to break out of the circle of relations described by Sartre in *Being and Nothingness*. To be bored is to enjoy a distance from both the threat and the temptation of the look. In boredom, one realizes one's own free involvement in the situation, and this realization releases the magical hold of the other.

Thus, it seems, the yawn is a hole with a difference, for it can swallow the subjectivity of the look. At the same time, it does not invite filling the way that other holes do. There is something empty and yet full about the yawn. It is indeed a hole but one that is full and expressive: it is a hole that overflows itself. Sartre indicates this, I believe, by frequently connecting the bored yawn with tears: "I give such a big yawn that tears come into my eyes,"[24] and "From time to time I yawn so widely that tears roll down my cheeks."[25]

I conclude, then, that the examined life of an existentialist may not and need not always be as exciting as those of us threatened by the recognition of freedom might think. This does not, however, mean that an authentic life is not worth living. It only means that we can become bored with our own freedom and with that of others and that boredom, or at least the constant possibility thereof, must play an important role in an ethics of authenticity developing out of the thought of Sartre.

## NOTES

1 Jean-Paul Sartre, *Nausea*, trans. Lloyd Alexander (Norfolk, Conn.: New Directions Books, 1959), p. 26.

2 *Ibid.*, p. 210.

3 *Ibid.*

4 *Ibid.*, pp. 176-77.

5 *Ibid.*, pp. 171-72.

6 *Ibid.*, pp. 108, 122, 134-36.

7 *Ibid.*, p. 29.

8 *Ibid.*, p. 19.

9 Jean-Paul Sartre, "Existentialism Is a Humanism," *Existentialism from Dostoevsky to Sartre*, ed. Walter Kaufmann (New York: The World Publishing Company, 1963), pp. 292-99.

10 *Being and Nothingness*, trans. Hazel E. Barnes (New York: Philosophical Library, 1956), p. 56.

11 Søren Kierkegaard, *Either/Or*, Vol. I, trans. David F. Swenson and Lillian Marvin Swenson (Garden City, New York: Doubleday & Company, Inc., 1959), p. 24.

12 *Ibid.*, p. 25.

13 *Ibid.*, p. 36.

14 *Ibid.*, p. 281.

15 *Ibid.*, p. 282.

16 *Either/Or*, Vol. II, trans. Walter Lowrie (Garden City, New York: Doubleday & Company, Inc., 1959), p. 352.

17 See the account of Judge William in William Earle, "The Paradox and Death of God," *Christianity and Existentialism*, William Earle, James M. Edie, John Wild (Evanston: Northwestern University Press, 1963), p. 73.

18 *The Sickness Unto Death*, trans. Walter Lowrie (Garden City, New York: Doubleday & Company, Inc., 1954), p. 203.

19 Sartre, *Being and Nothingness*, p. 580, in contrasting the spirit of seriousness with play, notes that the serious man "...does not even imagine any longer the possibility of *getting out of* the world...."

20 *Ibid.*, p. 581.

21 Sartre, *Saint Genet*, trans. Bernard Frechtman (New York: The New American Library, 1964), p. 626.

22 *Nausea*, p. 11.

23 *Ibid.*, p. 122.

24 *Ibid.*, p. 45.

25 *Ibid.*, p. 210.

# Contributors

HAZEL E. BARNES is Professor Emeritus of Philosophy, University of Colorado. She has translated Sartre's *Being and Nothingness* and *Search for a Method*. She has written numerous books and articles on literature and philosophy, both classical and contemporary. Among her many books are *Humanistic Existentialism: The Literature of Possibility* and *The Meddling of the Gods: Four Essays on Classical Themes* (University of Nebraska Press); *An Existentialist Ethics* and *Sartre and Flaubert* (University of Chicago Press).

LINDA BELL is Professor of Philosophy, Georgia State University. She has written articles on existentialism and ethics, including "Sartre, Dialectic, and the Problem of Overcoming Bad Faith" (*Man and World*), and "Sartre, Alienation, and Society" (*Philosophy and Social Criticism*). She is also the author of *Sartre's Ethics of Authenticity* (University of Alabama Press), and the editor of *Visions of Women* (Humana Press).

JOSEPH S. CATALANO is Professor of Philosophy, Kean College of New Jersey. He is the author of *A Commentary on Jean-Paul Sartre's "Being and Nothingness"* and *A Commentary on Jean-Paul Sartre's "Critique of Dialectical Reason"* (University of Chicago Press).

MAX CHARLESWORTH has been Reader in Philosophy and Chair of the Department of Philosophy, University of Melbourne, Australia. He is the author of *The Existentialists and Jean-Paul Sartre* (St. Martin's Press) and editor of *The Problem of Religious Language* (Prentice-Hall). He is also the editor of the journal *Sophia* (Australia).

KEITH HOELLER is Adjunct Professor of Psychology, Antioch University, Seattle, and editor of the *Review of Existential Psychology & Psychiatry*. He is the author of numerous articles in existential philosophy and psychology, and editor of *Merleau-Ponty and Psychology* and *Readings in Existential Psychology & Psychiatry* (Humanities Press).

SANDER H. LEE is Professor of Philosophy, Keen State College, University of New Hampshire. He is the author of "The Central Role of Universalization in a Sartrean Ethics" (*Philosophy and Phenomenological Research*), "Liberty, Equality and Fraternity in a Gandhian Society" (*Journal of Social Philosophy*), and "The Obligation of Society towards the Victims of Crime" (in *The Victims of Crime*, Charles C. Thomas, Publisher).

LUCIEN MALSON is the author of *Wolf Children and the Problem of Human Nature: The Wild Boy of Aveyron by Jean Itard* (Monthly Review Press).